Spiritual Awakening

Discover How to Detox Your Mind and Achieve Higher Consciousness through Kundalini Awakening and Reiki Healing. Learn the Concept of Lucid Dream, Your Gateway to the Inner Self

Chandra Wilbur

© Copyright 2021 - All rights reserved.

The content contained within this book may not be reproduced, duplicated or transmitted without direct written permission from the author or the publisher.

Under no circumstances will any blame or legal responsibility be held against the publisher, or author, for any damages, reparation, or monetary loss due to the information contained within this book. Either directly or indirectly.

Legal Notice:

This book is copyright protected. This book is only for personal use. You cannot amend, distribute, sell, use, quote or paraphrase any part, or the content within this book, without the consent of the author or publisher.

Disclaimer Notice:

Please note the information contained within this document is for educational and entertainment purposes only. All effort has been executed to present accurate, up to date, and reliable, complete information. No warranties of any kind are declared or implied. Readers acknowledge that the author is not engaging in the rendering of legal, financial, medical or professional advice. The content within this book has been derived from various sources. Please consult a licensed professional before attempting any techniques outlined in this book.

By reading this document, the reader agrees that under no circumstances is the author responsible for any losses, direct or indirect, which are incurred as a result of the use of information contained within this document, including, but not limited to, errors, omissions, or inaccuracies.

TABLE OF CONTENTS

INTRODUCTION 6
CHAPTER 1 STEPS FOR POSITIVE THINKING 8
CHAPTER 2 DETOX YOUR MIND 14
CHAPTER 3 TYPES OF SPIRITUAL AWAKENING 20
   Spiritual Awakening Examples 22
CHAPTER 4 SYMPTOMS AND SIGNS 26
   False Signs of Spiritual Awakening 29
CHAPTER 5 STAGES OF SPIRITUAL AWAKENING AND TIPS TO HELP YOUR THROUGH THEM 32
   Stage 1: A Calling From Within for Change 33
   Stage 2: Relearning Your Inner Journey 33
   Stage 3: Creating the Changes as You Step Into Your Power 34
CHAPTER 6 PREPARATION FOR AWAKENING 38
CHAPTER 7 SPIRITUAL AWAKENING TRIGGERS 44
CHAPTER 8 BLOCKERS FOR SPIRITUAL AWAKENING 48
CHAPTER 9 SPIRITUAL AWAKENING AND ANGER 54
CHAPTER 10 SPIRITUAL AWAKENING AND ANXIETY 58
   Learning to Meditate for Anxiety 59
CHAPTER 11 THE AFTER-EFFECTS OF AWAKENING 64
CHAPTER 12 PROS AND CONS OF SPIRITUAL AWAKENING 70
   Pros 70
   Cons 73
CHAPTER 13 HOW TO REMOVE NEGATIVITY AND CLEAN AURA .. 76
CHAPTER 14 HOW TO BALANCE YOUR CHAKRAS 82
   Nourishing Your Chakras 86
CHAPTER 15 KUNDALINI YOGA: ASANAS, PRANAYAMA, MUDRAS, MANTRAS 90
   Asanas 92
   Pranayama 93
   Mudras 93
   Mantras 94

CHAPTER 16 KUNDALINI ENERGY 96

CHAPTER 17 REIKI HEALING 102
How Reiki Healing Works: The Theory 102
How Reiki Healing Is Done: The Healing Session 105

CHAPTER 18 SPIRITUAL AWAKENING VS. KUNDALINI AWAKENING: WHAT'S THE DIFFERENCE 108
The Main Differences Between Spiritual Awakening and Kundalini Awakening 110

CHAPTER 19 SPIRITUAL AWAKENING VS. ENLIGHTENMENT 112

CHAPTER 20 BREATHING TECHNIQUES 118

CHAPTER 21 GUIDED MEDITATION FOR BEGINNERS 124
What Meditation Really Is 124
Meditation 101: The Passive Mind 125
Third Eye Visualization Meditation 128

CHAPTER 22 THIRD EYE ACTIVATION 130

CHAPTER 23 LUCID DREAMS: WHAT ARE AND HOW TO EXPERIENCE THEM 136
Guided Meditations for Lucid Dreams 139

CHAPTER 24 ASTRAL PROJECTION FOR BEGINNERS 142

CHAPTER 25 THE FACETS OF AWAKENING 150
The Facet of Mind 150
The Facet of Self 151
The Facet of Spiritual Energy 152
The Facet of Universal Consciousness 152
The Facet of True Reality 154

CHAPTER 26 LEARN MORE ABOUT THE CHAKRAS 156

CHAPTER 27 BENEFITS OF REIKI 162
Benefits of Reiki 162

CONCLUSION 168

Chandra Wilbur

Introduction

Have you ever felt a strange sort of awareness? One that isn't quite conscious of its own existence, but is present at the same time? That's what spiritual awakening feels like. It's an experience where you come to know yourself as a whole for the first time. You redefine your own existence by learning how to exist in a state of peace and love with every facet of yourself. It's something that's hardly ever talked about because it's very hard to put into words. But it is the most amazing thing you'll ever experience.

Spiritual awakening is a state of self-realization that expands a person's conscious awareness. Many people falsely associate "spiritual awakening" with religion. Spiritual awakening is not about going to church or being a part of any organized religion. It's about realizing your place in the world and how you fit into the world around you and accepting those roles. When you're in an awakened state, it's like everything around you is moving in slow motion. Things are clear and there is no confusion or tension in any aspect of your life.

To better understand spiritual awakening, we also have to grasp its connection to the chakras. Chakras are often referred to as "energy centers." They are essentially focal points of energy in the body, each having its own function, purpose, and color. These qualities are then transferred to the body's aura. There are seven major chakras that correspond to the colors of the rainbow: red, orange, yellow, green, blue, indigo and violet. When these chakras are balanced and working properly, they increase one's spiritual awareness and allow for greater personal growth. As such, learning how to balance the chakras is helpful to achieve spiritual awakening.

Many people also acknowledge the importance of reiki healing in spiritual awakening and many people who practice reiki are finding that this healing art has the unique ability to positively impact their spirituality, as well as their emotional, mental, and physical health. The principles of reiki may be ancient in origin but they still apply in today's modern world. Reiki is a form of energy healing that involves laying on hands and using gentle tapping techniques to heal illnesses and help balance spiritual energies. It can also be used for self-improvement through guided meditation, visualization, and visualizations of plants or animals.

Beginners often get overwhelmed on how to experience spiritual awakening but one way to address this is through meditation. A lot of people know that meditation has a huge number of health benefits, but not everyone is aware of the spiritual side of meditation. There are a lot of ways that can be read in the following pages as to how this can be utilized for spiritual awakening.

On the other hand, spiritual awakening is also associated with lucid dreaming. In fact, lucid dreamers say that when one attains lucidity, they achieve a spiritual awakening. A lucid dream has been described as "the feeling of being completely aware while you are dreaming."

Despite the real and vivid experience of lucid dreaming, many people still question the validity of these claims so read along to discover its link to spiritual awakening.

Spiritual awakening can be achieved through various forms and methods but before one can do so, one has to learn its links and connections to other aspects such as kundalini awakening, yoga, astral projection, and the like.

Chapter 1
Steps for Positive Thinking

I know we have all been facing very challenging times in the world. We've all watched and been shocked at how people have responded to what's been going on in the world.

Studies regularly show that optimists are more likely to maintain better physical health than pessimists, including a 50% lower risk of cardiovascular disease and greater survival rates when fighting cancer.

A happy nature can help you get through the challenges that cloud every life. The question is, do individuals who perceive things with the glass half complete also delight in better health compared to the sad class who see it as half sufficient? Following a range of research from America and Europe, the answer is absolute.

Optimism aids individuals adapt to illnesses and convalesce from surgery. Even more fascinating is the effect of a good perspective on health and longevity in general. Studies convey that a positive perspective early in life can foretell better health and a lower rate of death during follow-up periods of 15 to 40 years.

In a particular research, doctors evaluated 309 middle-aged patients who were scheduled to undergo coronary artery bypass surgery. In addition to a complete preoperative physical exam, each client experienced a psychological test formulated to measure positivity, anxiety, neuroticism, and self-confidence. The researchers examined all the clients for 6 months after surgery. When they assessed the results, they discovered that those who were positive were only half as likely as pessimists to demand re-hospitalization. In a similar study of two hundred ninety-eight angioplasty patients, positivity was also protective; over six months, pessimists were three times more likely than optimists to have heart attacks or require repeat angioplasty or bypass operations. Optimistic people were more compassionate and caring. The reality is there is a collective consciousness and a collective unconscious. When the whole world is going through times like this and watching the news and hearing negative stories, it's very easy to slip into darkness. We can feel the shadows and get depressed and frustrated. I'm going to give you some ways you can get back to your center, back to a wonderful state of peace inside. There are ways to stay strong and in a positive state of mind. There are tools that you can use to overcome negativity. This is an important time to use your inner tools you may have learned to help overcome negativity. Staying positive is so important to your health in your state of mind.

Here are a few things we'll be going over.

1. Gratitude, gratitude, gratitude, gratitude. When you stop and are grateful for what you've got, you change your health, and you change your state of mind. Begin to go from the negative to the positive. Gratitude will make you happy, even if you're depressed.

2. Listen to music. Music has been proven to release dopamine; it changes your brain waves. I love music, and I have to say, music for me lifts me, inspires me, and changes my state of mind. It's a wonderful tool.

3. Walk-in nature. They say if you just walk for 50 minutes, you can change your mood. You also can change your energy level. You start to see the good in life. You can practice gratitude as you're walking, and you can even listen to music and practice gratitude as you're walking, which I do. What a powerful combination. I always feel better after a walk.

4. Do yoga. Yoga is a wonderful way to go bring your body, mind, and spirit together. It's a way to be in the highest union with God while you're in your body. Your body loves to exercise, and again, it changes your chemical makeup. You can do it in your home if you're staying

inside. If you have a backyard, it's a bonus. It's even better to do it in the sun. Yoga is a wonderful tool.

5. Another wonderful tool is doing something creative. When you're in that creative flow, you allow that inspiration to come in, and it changes your whole state of mind. You could draw, write a poem, or even start a book that you've meant to write. That creative nature is the most positive energy tool that can help others and be in union with the source of all creation.

6. Read a good book. There's nothing like curling up with a good book. It's great to retreat into a very good book and read something positive and learn something. Reading a book is a great thing to do.

7. Talk to a friend or family member. When you talk to a friend or loved one, it's similar to going to a psychiatrist or psychologist. It's nice to talk to someone positive, of course not someone who's going to bring you down and complain.

8. Talking to a loved one can be a way of releasing your hidden fears and getting your thoughts out. You realize you're not alone. Supporting each other and having a wonderful energy exchange is such a great gift.

9. Smile! Smiling can change the way you feel. It can change your state of mind. Take a moment right now and smile. I first learned this from a meditation retreat with Thich Nat Hanh at the Sonoma Mountain Zen Center. During meditation, he said, smile and it made a difference. I remember how surprised I was when he said that in meditation because I had not heard a meditation teacher say that before. I was able in that meditation to see the effects of smiling.

10. Another wonderful tool is helping another person. Helping others with compassion and an act of kindness is a simple thing and very effective. Acts of kindness make you feel good. It helps spread that positive energy

to another person. That can get paid forward, and it can have an amazing ripple effect.

11. Breathe. Conscious breathing is truly a great gift that can instantly make a difference. Remember, Breath Sweeps Mind—my Zen teacher. Bill Kwong Roshi, the founder of the Sonoma Mountain Zen Center, wrote this years ago. "Breath sweeps mind," and he wrote it in calligraphy. I still keep it to this day. And it's true. Your breath actually can change your state of mind; it does. If you find that you are getting into a funk or getting depressed, you can stop that with conscious breathing. We will be doing some breathing coming up here soon. You see how it works.

12. Affirmations, Prayers, and Meditation. All practices are the keys to staying positive. The most important affirmations and meditation are such an amazing way to get rid of any negative energy and truly change your state of mind into a positive state of mind. It connects you with your inner resource. It connects you with your soul that connects you with God, to connect you with light; it connects you with love; it connects you with all good things. It's not just me saying this. The Mayo Clinic says, 'When you meditate, and when you keep your mind positive, you have an increased life span, you lower the rate of depression, you lower levels of distress. You have greater resistance to the common cold. You are a better psychological and physical being. You have cardiovascular health and a reduced risk of death from cardiovascular disease. You also have better-coping skills during hardships and times of stress.' I think we're in that hardship and times of stress situation at this time. In my entire life, I've never seen so many challenging things happening.

13. Take a news break. It's so important. Yes, stay aware of what's going on, and there are many ways to do that. But if you could have a half-hour of meditating or a half-hour of watching the news, which one would make you

feel better. If you take that time to meditate, you will feel better. How often have you found yourself watching the news and buying into the fear? You can find yourself even really in the course of half an hour of watching a newscast on TV getting pretty upset.

14. Clear your mind of fear. If you have fears, they can take root in your mind, and you have to clear them out. I suggest a very powerful white light around you, a brilliant white light to keep yourself protected from negative energy and to keep yourself protected from anything. Put a gorgeous, beautiful, extended white light around you and surround that white light with gold and light.

15. Visualize! See yourself staying positive and open to only the highest good, and say to yourself: I choose to hold the highest and the best vision for myself and all of humanity. I choose to hold the highest and the best vision for myself and all of humanity. I choose to stay positive and to believe in the good in humanity. I choose to remember this too shall pass. For indeed it will.

16. Compassion and love. We have to remember that light at the end of the tunnel. We do need to have more compassion for those who are struggling and suffering now. We can show our intention to have more love and more compassion to help other people. Have more compassion and love for yourself. Love is a great way to overcome fear.

17. You can choose to fully live your life and happiness and not fall prey to that fear's negative energy. Be grateful with that attitude of gratitude. That does help you to feel better, and it boosts your immunity by being positive.

18. Follow only the advice from those professionals who have clear and true help that you can use. Delete and repel anything that attempts to take you away from your good and for all of humanity. Hold that vision.

Chapter 2
Detox Your Mind

Many people are winding up with chronic conditions daily from among the dirty toxins in their environment, and they don't even know it. The products we use every day create a toxic mess on our minds, and that is one reason why many people suffer from anxiety, depression, poor performance at work, or lack of well-being.

Through most of the process of unfoldment, a great percentage of time may be spent unconsciously tuned to the frequencies of mind as we release and resolve identifications, little by little. The frequency classes of mind start at the bottom with very low-frequency emotions such as hate or depression and low frequencies of thought such as "I am a loser" or "Nobody likes me." These low frequencies have no direct benefits to the body; they are almost entirely disharmonious. By contrast, in the higher frequencies of emotion, such as personal love or self-confidence, and in the higher frequencies of thought such as "I am happy" or "I am loved" we are still tuned to the mind but with less disharmony. We would at least like to be in the higher frequencies of mind as much as possible so that leaping to consciousness does not present such a challenge. For this reason, we must address certain seeds of darkness that frequently complicate the process of tuning to consciousness.

Every day, you breathe in toxic chemicals that are unavoidable in our everyday environment, from household cleaners to insecticides. You can also breathe in these toxins while at work and even if you don't have a job. When you are eating away at your desk or dealing with someone over the phone, your body is absorbing all kinds of airborne toxins without you even knowing it.

Problems from toxins can cause damage to your brain that leads to a variety of mental illnesses and causes debilitating effects on your overall health. There is a limited amount of attention in the world about how toxic substances affect our body and mind, but the truth is that these chemicals can be responsible for mental health issues such as anxiety, depression, and behavioral problems.

Only one percent of what we breathe in gets evacuated via our lungs. The other 99 percent stays inside your body and creates havoc throughout your body. Once toxic substances enter your body, they will stay there for a long time because they will not be removed by your liver or kidneys very easily. There are many types of toxins that you breathe in every day, and the worst part is that they all affect your brain. You may have noticed that you are stressed out more than ever before, or you can't perform at work, or you don't feel the same anymore. These symptoms may be caused by toxic exposure overload.

When you are exposed to toxins daily, it will have an immediate effect on your health. Toxic substances affect the chemicals in your brain that control your emotions and behavior, and this affects your self-esteem and mental health. Both men and women are affected by toxins that they breathe into their bodies every day. Studies have been done that show that women's brains function differently from those of men's, which is why females experience symptoms such as anxiety, depression, behavioral problems, and much more.

There is still a great deal of mystery surrounding the effects of toxins on the brain, but it is known that many people who have chemicals build up in their bodies eventually lose their minds. This is why it is important to detox your mind and cleanse your body from all these toxic substances that you are exposed to every day. To detox your mind, you need to do some deep breathing exercises daily. You have to learn how your brain works so that you can learn how your body works. You need to know which of your brain chemicals can cause anxiety and depression, and how those chemicals react with each other in a way that causes your brain to accept the various thoughts you have that create emotional problems. When you breathe in toxins, they stay for up to a long time in your body and brain.

The more toxins you inhale, the worse your health condition will be as a whole. People who have brain trauma from past illnesses or accidents are at a higher risk of having toxic overload problems. When you try to live in a world that is full of poisonous chemicals, this will cause flammable brain cells that will result in neurochemical imbalances in your brain that will eventually affect your health, behavior, and emotions. Your judgment will be affected. You will have poor decision-making abilities and low self-esteem.

By detoxing your mind, you are performing your body a great service. It is important to learn how to live in our world without adding more toxins into your system, especially before it becomes too late for you to do anything about it. The best way to detox your mind is by exercising daily and eating healthy foods. The more natural foods that you eat, the better off you will be in the long run. You will be able to sleep better, breathe easier and enjoy life a lot more if you cleanse your body from all the nasty toxins that you have been exposed to.

You have to make your body work better by removing the trash in your body and cleaning it out for good. Eliminating toxic substances from your system is important because they will only cause more major problems to your health and wellbeing. You can potentially live a healthier lifestyle if you detoxify your body from all the toxins that are causing your health problems. You will have a better life if you eliminate toxic chemicals from your body. Detoxing your mind is very important and it needs to be done daily so that you don't have a big problem on the road ahead. If you are not doing this, then all those toxins will turn into something that no one likes to think about, and this will be quite dangerous for your health. The toxins that you inhale daily are entering your body and will stay there for a long time. The longer they stay in your body, the more damage they will cause to your overall health. The more they stay inside you, the worse it will be for you.

If you are not taking responsibility for removing these toxins from your body, then it is going to be very difficult to live a healthy life. You will experience a lot of problems if you do not do anything about your toxic overload.

We're living in a tech-mad, quasi-adrenalized world. Sooner or later, it's bound to catch up with us. There are ways we can forestall the inevitable and mitigate some of the damage; and no, it doesn't involve meditation. Here are five ways of detoxifying your mind in this toxic age of ours.

Switch Off

We've all noticed how compulsive the average smartphone or tablet user is. And it's not just the electromagnetic radiation but being "connected" in a quasi-addictive way. Techno-activists will say that you can carry on using your handheld devices yet be mindful of the world around you and controlling your attention. That's a good way to meditate. The rest of us, and we're the majority, are likely to be so busy keeping up with the Joneses that we just live for those little micro-interactions. Simply put, we're addicted.

Realize That Your Thoughts Are Not You

Literally, religious faith is no longer mandatory for human salvation; nowadays people can be saved in all sorts of ways. But it still helps to believe in something a little larger than yourself. This is why it's important to remember that your thoughts are not you and that your sensations are not you either. When you notice that you're thinking negative thoughts—and the human brain is far too busy thinking for any of us to avoid that—simply let it go. You don't have to watch those thoughts as they pass by and waiting for them to go away naturally doesn't always work.

Meditate

It sounds simple, but meditation—the real thing, not those fashionable fads that are doing the rounds—is still the easiest and best way of calming down and learning to let go. And it doesn't necessarily require a religious or spiritual master. There are plenty of free guided meditations on YouTube or with your favorite mindfulness app.

Move

Nothing is stopping you from going for a long hike, an evening jog, or a swim. Not only will it keep your body in shape but also your mind, which is ultimately the same thing. In fact, being around nature—trees, mountains, and all that green stuff—has an amazing detoxifying effect on the mind. There shouldn't be a need to mention that it also helps with stress relief and depression.

Meditate on The Reality of Death

It's tough to think about death. Unless you're religious or superstitious, you know it's not in your future. But like being addicted to a phone—or that other bad habit—thinking too much about the inevitable can cause depression, or worse. Death by overthinking is no different from dying of any other illness. If you have a family member who has just passed away, do what you can to make the time that they were alive special and meaningful for them and those around them. The same goes for yourself; don't think about when you'll die because it's not worth it.

It might sound rather grim, but in fact, there's plenty of light and laughter to find in life. Just because we're conscious of the way we feel doesn't mean that we have to be miserable—we just have to accept ourselves as we are. When you get down to basics, everything is pretty simple. The mind is a muscle, and it needs exercise regularlyT.

Chapter 3
Types of Spiritual Awakening

Spiritual awakening is a term that is very often used to describe a personal spiritual journey of self-discovery and transformation. Awakening may be experienced through dreams, visions, spiritual feelings, or a series of physical events. Sensations vary between the individual and can depend upon whether the person has an open mind or a closed heart.

While there are numerous types of awakening it is important to understand that each person's experience will be unique in part due to their past experiences as well as current life circumstances. Examples of the types of spiritual awakenings an individual may experience are:

1. Emotional or physical trauma. Trauma causes a person to undergo a life-changing event resulting in a healing response from the body/mind. The mind and body respond to intense fear, pain, anger, or grief by causing one to become very still and quiet so that healing can occur.

2. Spiritual crisis. It is a difficult event that leads to a more open awareness or being more spiritually aware of how life is felt. The individual in this situation will often seek out help or advice to move forward in their spiritual growth.

3. Soul Awakening. A person experiences a spiritual awareness that has altered their life as well as their view on life completely. In many cases, this can result from major life challenges such as physical crises, divorce, death, major career transitions, etc.

4. Regeneration. When the ego dies and is transformed into a more spiritual part of self, the individual will often

experience a deep sense of happiness and joy, allowing for new life changes to occur in their life.

5. Awakening into Spirit. This type of awakening can occur as part of spiritual healing or as a result of an actual physical event where one has taken on a different solid form to interact with others.

6. Miraculous healing. In this type of awakening, it is the body that experiences change resulting from the mind's awareness of pain and frustration.

Many people enter into a spiritual journey to become more open and aware of their spirituality to have a deeper connection with God, Jesus, Sananda/Ra/Kuan Yin, etc. While this can be a positive experience for some it does not mean that everyone entering into this journey will be led there by an outside force (god or spirit). Spiritual awakening can occur for many reasons and is not always triggered by a specific spiritual experience or event. The individual may awaken to part of their soul's purpose, a dream they had and hope to fulfill, or through an actual physical event as described above. Spiritual awakening may also be spontaneous or through the help of spiritual guides. Because one's experience will be unique it is important to talk with others about their experiences to receive support during the journey of self-discovery. Individuals who are dedicated to finding and understanding their soul's purpose may experience an awakening as part of the process. An awakening will occur when the individual's spiritual body is ready to change into its next stage of development. These changes may be karmic in nature, requiring the individual to work through past life experiences while also learning from them for their current life. Soul awakening, or spiritual transformation, occurs when an individual's soul awakens from its slumber and causes a change in behavior or personality. Soul awakening is a transformation that occurs when a person's soul separates from the body. The soul usually remains connected to the body for several years following the birth or until its death, before being freed from the physical constraints of the physical world and moving into a state of unity with God, or other spiritual beings which may be God's messenger on Earth.

The separation between the physical and spiritual bodies is often gradual and incomplete—as in cases of near-death experiences.

Suffering Soul Awakening

Soul awakening is the experience that occurs when one's soul falls away from the body after death and remains connected to it for several years or until death. It is also a form of spiritual rebirth. The soul may then be transformed into a spiritual being while its physical body undergoes decomposition, this process usually ending approximately one year following death.

Spiritual Awakening

A spiritual awakening can be the result of a traumatic experience that causes one to gain a new understanding of the purpose of life or their own soul's journey. It is common for individuals who have undergone a spiritual awakening to have an increased desire to improve themselves personally. The process of spiritual awakening may cause the individual to become more interested in spirituality and personal development, oftentimes leading them to books or classes dedicated to these topics.

Spiritual awakening is a period of change or transformation which occurs as the result of a serious emotional challenge or a life crisis. The individual will awaken to personal responsibility and their ability to determine the outcome of their life, no longer being held back by fear and/or guilt. While some may find this new ability to be scary, many people begin using it to become more successful in their personal and professional lives.

Spiritual Awakening Examples

A spiritual awakening can be the result of intense anger or grief. When a person experiences an intense emotion such as anger or grief, the mind often acts as if it were also experiencing that emotion. In many cases, it is when the individual is experiencing an intense emotional event such as grief, anger, or a major life event that they will begin to spiritually awaken via spiritual crisis. This can be a very intense and painful process for the individual; however, it can also bring them to a new life experience that they never thought was possible.

Kundalini Awakening

Kundalini awakening is a phenomenon where people experience intense spiritual and physical sensations due to the rise of Kundalini energy. It is believed to happen most often during periods of high stress, meditation, or other practices that work with the chakras.

Kundalini awakening is described as a feeling of intense warmth that begins at the base of the spine and rises up through the body. People report feeling powerful energy throughout their body, sometimes so much they need to move their body to reduce tension. Kundalini awakening can cause a wide range of physical manifestations, such as shaking, intense heat or cold, vibrations or spasms through the body, ringing in the ears (tinnitus), visions, or out-of-body experiences. This can be very frightening for the person experiencing it, it is sometimes considered a medical emergency. The Kundalini awakening experience is supposed to be a positive thing, some people report feeling an intense sense of love and peace, others report getting a vision or message from a spirit or God, but in about 10% of cases it can get stuck and become something called 'Kundalini syndrome.' When Kundalini energy gets stuck people can become paranoid, delusional, or aggressive. The person may need to be institutionalized and, if the episode is prolonged, they may even become suicidal.

Kundalini awakening is a concept from Yoga, and it is a serious spiritual issue that should not be attempted without proper guidance. There are many reports of people getting injured or even killed by "attempting" Kundalini awakening alone. Many people believe that Kundalini energy is dormant at birth but can be awakened through various practices such as meditation, yoga, or energy work. Most texts on Kundalini awakening recommend practicing a slow and steady approach to raising energy through the chakras, monitoring your energy levels, and adjusting practices as necessary. This ensures that your body can handle the increased energy and that you are ready for the in-depth spiritual experiences that are supposed to accompany Kundalini awakening.

Third-Eye Awakening

Many people in the Western world are undergoing a period of regeneration of consciousness that is characterized by the birth of new, unique ideas, which usually manifest as some type of social change or spiritual awakening. We have seen this phenomenon at every turn in history: from the Age of Enlightenment (early 18th century) to the Great French Revolution and even to present-day human awakening (21st century). This process is often referred to as "The Third-eye Awakening" or "The Shift." The Third-eye Awakening is a powerful and positive energetic event that increasingly impacts the collective consciousness to address unresolved negative emotions and conditions. It also signals the end of a cycle and the beginning of something new, from which a new era emerges with a new paradigm. This can happen in both personal lives, as well as to nations, societies, and civilizations.

Throughout history, there have been many such events. The most famous of these is the "Age of Enlightenment" (17th and 18th centuries) when the scientific revolution occurred. After this, we saw the French Revolution in 1789, and shortly afterward war and violence around the world. In recent times, we have experienced moments when people have awakened to their true spiritual nature—like the hippies on the cover of Sgt. Pepper's Lonely Hearts Club Band, or the San Francisco Renaissance as told in Don Quixote. And of course, we now have the new generation of lightworkers and awakened ones who are actively uplifting Gaia and humanity.   Today, "The Shift" is reaching its peak as most people are on their own personal path of spiritual development. This starts with the belief that there is a higher power (God) working alongside them, combined with an increased interest in spirituality and self-realization. A clear sign of this shift is that many people are searching for religious beliefs that formerly were not part of their lives.

Mystical Awakening

If you've ever heard of the Principles of Thought or the 7 Planes, then you're well on your way to understanding what mystical awakening is. The idea that we are all one in a sequential series of planes or dimensions is an old one, and these principles have become central to many religions and philosophical traditions. Mystical awakening often results in a sense of unity with everything around us because it puts us in touch with our true spiritual selves.

"The Three Voices"

Mystical awakening often brings about the sense that we are "not of this world," that we have returned to our natural state. It is a blending of every possible human experience into one. This is expressed with the idea of "The Three Voices." The Three Voices are:

The Image of Silence (the Witness which is the presence or awareness of everything), the Voice of Knowledge (the source of understanding and wisdom about everything), and the Voice of Power (the force that drives all creation forward, whether it be through love or through greed).

The Mystical Awakened Person hears these voices as they go about their daily lives but also knows that they are on an ever-evolving path towards growth and self-discovery.

Chapter 4
Symptoms and Signs

Authentic Sign 1: Increased Emotional Wellbeing

One of the major hindrances of spiritual awakening is the emotional disruption we experience sometimes. If you are truly spiritually awakened, the emotional wounds and trauma from your past would be healed which enables you to feel more genuine. Re-engaging the normal flow of positive emotions plays a pivotal role in every facet of our lives. Instead of being downtrodden or possessed by numerous archetypes, you tend to be more of an authentic and compassionate human. With greater emotional wellbeing, you develop less resistance to fight negativities you once resisted. Instead of shying away from reality, you embrace it and squarely confront anger, fear, and guilt.

Authentic Sign 2: Constant Reflection—Stopping and Seeing

To notice the authentic signs of spiritual awakening, it is imperative you 'pause' and have a moment of sober reflection. Looking back in a bid to understand the present is a luxury that our modern-day lives barely affords us. Due to the fast-paced society we live in, moments of reflection have been shortchanged for the excessive drive for success, achievement, and peak performance. When you find yourself bidding your time more often, reflecting back more often, chances are that you are truly spiritually awakened. During your moments of reflection, your intuition and inner impulse drive you clearly understand the present. Reflection essentially helps you to access memories from your subconscious. However, this self-reflective moment isn't judgmental, or biased, as the spirit is although curious—it is unbiased.

Authentic Sign Three 3: Positive Change in Character

Probably the most obvious and authentic sign of spiritual awakening is seen in your character. Behaviors such as greed, ego, and addiction to bad habits are fully discarded. Your Higher Self no longer has the tendencies to behave like the lower soul or strive to need basic needs. When you realize you aren't truly lost but you're whole and complete you tend to become less reactive towards basic needs and negativities around you. A good sign of spiritual awakening is the feeling of completeness, and genuinely being part of the whole from moment to moment.

Authentic Sign 4: Merging the Opposites

Due to the rigid fundamentalist belief of some people, they have a clear-cut distinction between black and white, male and female, good and bad, left and right... and the list goes on. As humans, we are often pushed to completely do away with the opposite side and exclusively stick with the side that suits us. Dissociating from one of the pair seems to have resolved the tension our ego face, but honestly, it has only reinforced our shadow self. If you effectively merge the opposites within you, resolving the tension in your ego—it is a clear indication of spiritual awakening.

Authentic Sign Five 5: Transformation of Inner Self

On average, everyone's waking state is preoccupied with ego, based almost exclusively on personal achievement, money, family, friends, and the outer world in general. A good sign of spiritual awakening is when you notice a paradigm shift from the outer world to your inner thoughts, dreams, and feelings.

Authentic Sign 6: Change in Values and Priorities

Spiritual awakening essentially causes a change in values and priorities from the regular Do and Don't lay out by religion to the development of an ethical framework based on an awakened individual's perception. Discarded the moral code and ethics provided by others and embracing what's best for the moment is a clear indication of spiritual awakening. The paradigm shift towards values of our Higher Self is one of the reasons why our behavior changes during spiritual awakening. Your regular values such as materialistic achievements are substituted for 'being values' such as self-sufficiency, perfection, beauty, truth, and wholeness.

Authentic Sign 7: Increased Sense of Personal Responsibility

A feeling to be more honest with yourself emanates when you begin to find more authority in your inner self. At the point where you cannot tolerate the shadow side anymore, spiritual awakening may be on the horizon. Exhibiting a great sense of accountability and personal responsibilities for your words, thoughts, and actions, points towards spiritual awakening. Of course, if you cannot be held responsible for your personal life, then you are not accountable. In the absence of accountability, the feeling of guilt is completely eliminated. However, spiritual awakening makes you feel guilt for your bad actions and gives you the drive to correct yourself.

Authentic Sign 8: Experience of Inner Freedom and Deep Sense of Satisfaction

Ego is one of our major sources of fear, desire for materialistic achievements, and tension to succeed. When the ego has been tossed aside, there's an inherent sense of satisfaction and inner freedom regardless of the happenings around us. When you are spiritually awakened, you tend to be more relaxed into yourself which provides you the much-needed inner freedom you always sought after in the external world.

Authentic Sign 9: General Change in Lifestyle

Another major sign of true spiritual awakening is the consciousness and betterment of your lifestyle. Most of the behavior you put up normally before becomes unacceptable to you. The behaviors you would exhibit will be of the Higher Self, devoid of egoistic cravings.

Authentic Sign 10: Deep Sense of Oneness and Wholeness

When your ego has effectively been dealt with, it fears for its existence and barely clings on to life. The Higher Spirit has no fear of being ignored or separated from. The Spirit doesn't work with race, gender, or nationality. More so, the spirit exists outside space and time, and as such death is an irrelevant concept for it.

Spiritual awakening is a term often used to describe the process of personal growth in which one is transformed through life experiences and self-inquiry. This can happen to anyone, at any time, and it's not dependent on any specific belief or religion. When you experience spiritual awakening, it changes your perspective on the world and your place in it.

"Transformed beyond recognition" is an apt description of spiritual awakening, because it happens to everyone differently. You may not know what exactly caused it except that suddenly you feel like something happened (or didn't happen).

One does not need to be religious or a believer in any particular spirituality to experience a spiritual awakening. Even atheists and agnostics can undergo spiritual awakenings.

False Signs of Spiritual Awakening

Before we look at the authentic signs of spiritual awakening, let's consider some common false signs.

False Sign 1: Assuming you're 'All Good' and Others Are 'All Evil.'

This is one of the most common signs of false spiritual awakening. The belief in self-perfection is deeply ingrained in most of us. To be truly spiritually awakened, you must uproot this false belief. You will know you have successfully discarded such false beliefs when you quit passing judgment on others but instead seeing everyone as an integral part of the universe.

False Sign 2: False Belief of Self-Spirituality

Falsely identifying yourself as a 'spiritual person' is a sign of false spiritual awakening and spiritual ego. Truthfully, if you are truly spiritually awakened, you would neither be materialistic or spiritual. Not only will you live above both materialism and spiritualism, but you would also incorporate both as part of your life.

False Sign 3: Acting 'All Innocent'

Pretending to be innocent and nice isn't a true sign of spiritual awakening but a pointer to psychological immaturity. At home, in religious gatherings, and various institutions, we are told by our parents or guardian to be nice. We often end up complying with this demand, which leads to reinforcement of our shadow side. Truth is, if you're acting all nice and innocent, chances are that you are still being manipulated by others.

False Sign 4: False Belief That You're Better Than Others

You must have observed a similar pattern among the false signs of spiritual awakening which dwells majorly on traps of ego inflation. Although spiritual awakening is supposed to make us more humane, some people use it as a tool to judge and dissociate. This false sign often occurs when you read a new book on spirituality, start a spiritual practice or find a spiritual teacher. You have to be careful whenever you feel you've 'arrived.' This belief may be a sign of psychological development other than spiritual awakening.

Chapter 5
Stages of Spiritual Awakening and Tips to Help Your Through Them

Your soul is asking for you to view the world around you with a new perspective. One that aligns with who it is that you are destined to become. But to enable this change of perspective, to become who you have always wanted to be, your whole world needs to be turned upside down—your understanding of yourself, your loved ones, your home life, maybe even your career. Such a drastic change in our life can create extreme confusion, for how are we meant to know how to solve such a demand, especially if our lives were already flowing in perfect harmony? But even if your life appeared as though everything was fine, there was something at the core level that needed to shift, something that needed to be changed so that the energy of your soul could evolve and transform into true greatness. And for this to take place, you need to unlearn what you thought you knew and relearn the truth of who you really are. We call this invitation for transformation a spiritual awakening because of two reasons:

1. Spiritual: Because you are now forced to gain a deeper connection with your soul and your reality to change your perception of life.

2. Awakening: Because it is as though you have awoken to a new way of life, a new perspective that you had never thought could be possible before; yet it had always existed, you have just now opened your eyes to see it for what it really is.

Navigating the spiritual awakening process may feel intimidating. You may feel at times that you cannot go on, that nothing is working out for you, that everything is going against you.

You may feel more inclined to recluse into depressive thoughts or anxious feelings—because at least then you could define what is going on in your life. You may spend a long time searching for answers that never seem to come, and you might be asking for help but it never arrives. This is the darkest part of the spiritual awakening process and yet this is still the beginning because once you learn what and how to change, you still need to implement these changes to take charge of your life.

Stage 1: A Calling From Within for Change

This is the invitation for transformation and it usually comes as the result of a traumatic event. Depression and anxiety are both mental health challenges that may arise from this experience, and if they do, we must focus on healing this energy as we would with any other healing. Stage one is all about learning "what" is happening to you, with a focus on trying to stabilize your emotions and feelings. It's feeling the energy shift within and around you without your control. It's a moment to tune into the emotions overflowing, realigning with your soul, and learning how to channel the wisdom from your intuition within.

Stage 2: Relearning Your Inner Journey

You've now healed the trauma, but you are craving a deeper meaning in your life. This stage signifies in-depth self-reflection in your journey of self-discovery. You will spend a lot of time following the seed questions of "Who am I?" "What am I doing?" "Where am I going?" Although you may have determined conclusions about these questions before, the event prior has enforced you to lose these beliefs. The second stage is a focus on "why" this is happening as you nurture your thirst for knowledge and fulfill your desire for a better life.

Stage 3: Creating the Changes as You Step Into Your Power

By now you have moved through the healing process and are open to learn how to live authentically and fully step into your power. You understand that the wisdom received in exchange for the trauma has shaped you most powerfully and you are eager to manifest the vision of your future self clearly while being proactive in taking steps to reach these goals. In the third stage, we are looking at "how" we can implement what we have learned consistently. We implement the changes into our lives to become the version of ourselves that our soul is craving.

We will explore each stage of the spiritual awakening process and learn journaling exercises and rituals to assist in the growth of your personal development journey. Remember to never be upset with yourself for taking a long time or wanting to move out of one stage into the next as everything is perfectly on time. You may not realize why you aren't going to the next stage even if you feel ready; remember that it's your Soul Contract taking charge of this decision. So just accept where you are right now, surrender your fears, and lean into the challenge. You are taking a giant leap down the spiral of your Soul Contract and jumping deeply into the growth of your soul.

Throughout your healing process, you need to remind yourself to shift the blame from "why is this happening to me" to "what is this here to teach me?" If the answers aren't coming through to you, have patience and know that the answers will come to you at the right time. We need to become comfortable with the unknown. We need to learn how to live with uncertainty and find peace within ourselves. The more time we spend contemplating over the past or worrying about our future, the more our souls are robbed of the joy of the present moment. If we look to the present moment, we find all the answers that we could ever need. We are surrounded by the wisdom of ancient ancestors that have passed on from generation to generation who hold the secrets of the Universe. From them, we learn the scientific formula of the creation of life that proves that nothing is by chance, everything is perfectly aligned, and it's because of this particular recipe of heat, water, atoms, and chemicals between the sun and Earth that life here is possible. Our planet could not survive had it been any closer or further away from the sun than it is now. We literally are a living miracle! What an incredible thought knowing that everything aligned perfectly in the Universe to enable life to form, and for you to be conceived. You are not here by accident. You are meant to be living this life! Everything in your world has happened for a reason. And that reason is for you to be here and share your authentic medicine with the world! Your spiritual awakening is the entry point to the greatest transformation you will ever encounter. The beginning will be the most difficult, and you may feel a bit of resistance, denial, and fear. You will know you have reached the middle when you have accepted your situation and are eager to learn how to heal and transition. And when you reach the final stage, you will know that you are healing, or have healed, but aren't able to clearly see the reasons why yet. What stage are you at? Accept where you are, get your journal to write some encouraging words about it. For example:

If You Are at the Beginning

I feel as though I have begun my spiritual awakening process. I am at the beginning and all I see is darkness. I am unsure how to find my way out. But I have faith that there is a way out. I know that this is all happening for a reason, even if I don't understand it right now. This phase in my life will pass, I just need to have patience, take care of myself, and be open to the guidance that will present itself to me.

If You Are in the Middle

I have learned to accept that this is part of my story. Although difficult and challenging as it may be, I know that in time I will be grateful for it. I've begun to experiment with new ways of healing, I've started listening to my body, my intuition, and I feel stronger because of it. The sadness is still with me on some days, but I can see that it's my own doing, for I am choosing to bring forth sad memories.

I am getting stronger in letting go, to surrender to the unknown, and each time that I do I feel carried by angelic energy. I know I am not alone and that gives me hope for better days.

I trust and believe that I am looked after by the divine Universe at all times. I know that this is a part of my Soul Contract; I just don't know the reason why. All I can do is have faith that all will be revealed when it is meant to.

If You Are Toward the End

I have passed the most difficult phase and I feel lighter today. There is still confusion around why this happened, but I know that the answers will come to me when the time is right.

I'm enjoying looking after my health in a new way, and I feel the connections around me more intensely. Sometimes they scare me, but then I remember that I am looked after by my Higher Self at all times. I do not worry or fear, because I have been through the worst now. It's only going to get better from here. I am ready to accept whatever may come my way with an open heart and a curious mind.

This is what it will feel like when you have moved through it:

- I see the world and everyone around me for what they truly are. I finally know the reasons why this happened. I am grateful for the experience, as difficult as it was; it has made me so strong, I didn't even know this kind of strength was possible. I didn't know these feelings of connection and love could be so profound. It's as though I am comprehending my existence, and divinity in an entirely new way.

- Each day you will get a bit better than the last, and even if you don't feel like you are getting better, trust and believe that it is happening. But you still need to do the work to move through this energy. A spiritual awakening has opened a new door for you, and this door has elevated your consciousness, it has opened your mind in a way that it has never been before. Every thought and feeling you are experiencing right now is valid, and you need to accept it so that you can move through it.

Before we learn how your life is going to change, I want to remind you of this useful technique to come back to at any time during your spiritual awakening process. This technique will help ground your soul into your body and call upon your Higher Self to come forth and appear.

Chapter 6
Preparation for Awakening

There isn't just one way your dormant energy becomes awakened. It can vary significantly from person to person. Some people practice yoga and meditation for years, working with Gurus before anything happens. For others, it can be completely spontaneous and caused by a buildup of traumatic situations, addictions, or significant loss or grief, whether or not the person has any former knowledge of what Kundalini even is. There is a myriad of stories like these which is why it's important to remain open-minded with yourself, but also all the other human souls looking for answers, or enlightenment. If you decided to read this book, you have already begun this journey. Knowing more about it can help you feel more aware of what is potentially ahead for you, or even someone you know. Preparing your mind, your body, and your spirit can be a great way to begin. Even if you have already experienced some of these things, this book can be a great resource for staying in balance or becoming more involved with the journey instead of letting it naturally unfold without any guidance or practice. Sometimes, when you let it unravel naturally, and don't practice any energy work, yoga, meditation, or other balancing or healing practices, the experience can feel more chaotic and uncomfortable, more disorienting and unpredictable.

Finding ways to nurture yourself through awakening is key to a joyful and fully opening experience.

Each fundamental part of yourself can go through some preparations to allow for a more intentional awakening. Like you read before, for some people, it can happen spontaneously, but chances are, if you are reading this book, you are interested in and excited about starting that process of awakening your Kundalini and knowing your divine truth.

The following are just some easy and convenient ways you can prepare your mind, body, and spirit to awaken.

Mind

1. Daily affirmation.

Examples:

- I am ready to align with my primal life force.
- I am one with the Universe and a part of All That Is.
- I have divine energy within me and I am ready to wake it up.
- I am open and accepting of everyone and everything.

You can always invent your mantras to suit your needs better but try to find ways to speak to yourself with the language and frequency of love. Say mantras first thing in the morning before work, while sitting in traffic, before bed, or any other time that feels appropriate.

Start practicing simple meditations, especially if you have never meditated before. Try not to overthink meditation. The fact is to clear the mind of thought, but if the thoughts come, let them and then see them pass away from you like an ocean wave or a cloud. You can even find guided meditations online if you are not ready to guide yourself. Just search "guided meditation" and find what feels right for you.

Practice the art of Mindfulness. The formal description of mindfulness is "a mental state acquired by focusing one's awareness on the present moment, while calmly acknowledging and accepting one's feelings, thoughts, and bodily sensations, used as a therapeutic technique." As it says, practice focusing your awareness on what is occurring for you in the present moment and follow that practice into the next moment. It could be as simple as focusing on every single moment you have while making a cup of tea, or every gesture, thought, and action involved in folding your laundry.

Body

1. Exercise. Subscribing to a gym and exercising every day is not necessary. You don't need to take aerobics classes or run 10 miles. Go for a walk around your neighborhood. Dance to a song you like in your living room. Tread water in a swimming pool. Go for a hike on the trail. Just move your body in some way that feels pleasant, that doesn't feel like work, and that simply allows you time to get your blood flowing.

2. Stretch. You don't have to stretch every day, but a couple of times a week is very beneficial. You can practice yoga poses, or you can find a wide variety of places to find stretching routines, online, in books, or in a dance class at a studio. One thing to keep in mind when you stretch: it is best to hold each stretch for a minute to a minute and a half. Your body needs the time to actually experience the result of the stretch. If you only, do it for ten seconds, there won't be much of a change in your muscles and tissues.

3. Eat well. Diet has a great impact on the way we feel and our energy. As part of Kundalini awakening, you may have a natural inclination to change your diet, which has been commonly reported. If you don't already, and to prepare for the experience ahead, start eating well by avoiding processed foods, alcohol, sugar, and large quantities of caffeine. Take it a step at a time if it's too much to do all at once. Eat more whole foods, vegetables, fruits, grains, lean meats, seeds. Drink a lot of water. Switch to tea instead of coffee. All of this will start preparing your body for the adventure ahead.

Spirit

1. Adopt a self-care practice. There are numerous approaches to do this. You can under the sun in the early daylight and soak in the warmth and glow, focusing on your energy channels and how they feel as you relax. Prepare a warm bath and add Epsom salt, preferred essential oils, and candlelight, and spend quality time in the water letting your muscles soak. Lean up against your favorite tree with your favorite book and your favorite snack for as long as you want. These are a few examples to try or create your own ideas that resonate with who you are. The goal is to give yourself permission to love and care for yourself.

2. Keep a dream journal. The subconscious mind communicates so much to us when we sleep. In ascension, as the Kundalini rises, many people report having very profound dreams, premonitions, contact with spirit guides, or astral travel experiences. Start keeping a dream journal to begin communicating with your dream world and your higher consciousness and look for messages from within.

3. Start a gratitude practice. It is proven that expressing gratitude, whether it be vocal, written down, or in the mind, can positively change your vibration frequency. The concept of gratitude is a part of living as an enlightened human being. You can keep it simple. Begin by saying or writing things like, "I am grateful to have shelter and food to eat." "I have gratitude for the job I have right now." "I am thankful to be a part of this world." And so on. The great thing is, it can be about anyone and anything. The point is that thankfulness and appreciation is a valuable practice that brings you into closer alignment with your divine power and ultimate transcendence.

Start practicing these things today! It will be a helpful way for you to prepare for the quality of life you are looking for as you seek awakening.

Chapter 7
Spiritual Awakening Triggers

Spiritual awakening triggers can be very complex and diverse. However, let us first go back to what spiritual awakening is. Spiritual awakening is not a common phenomenon, but it has happened to countless people across history. Indeed, it even happens today—even if it is rarer. So, what causes spiritual awakening? Can you come up with different factors that can potentially trigger a person's spiritual awakening and lead them to see that they have an inner spirit? Read on to find out!

Spiritual awakening is not something most people will experience in their lifetime. That said, some experience this phenomenon—though it does seem rarer nowadays than before. It appears that a lot of individuals today have lost touch with what their souls are like, or even the fact that they have a soul.

Well, those who do experience spiritual awakening also realize that they have a soul—and then realize how important this is to their lives and what it means for what happens in their lives. Their minds are broadened to new possibilities, and many of them start to seek more meaning in life than before. As such, they typically become more spiritual as well.   As spiritual awakening involves having the eyes of the soul opened—or at least recognizing their existence after being denied for so long—it is often followed by a sense of enlightenment or nirvana. Plus, many people who begin to awaken start to realize that there is more to them than just their physical body, and they start to see how everything fits into their lives—both physically and spiritually. As such, they typically become act much more positively in many ways—in all areas of their lives. In many ways, the spiritual awakening process is an amazing thing. It is usually quite difficult for most people to believe that they could be so spiritually awakened, and to come to terms with the fact that other things are going on in their lives besides just their physical body. However, those who do experience this often find that they start to see the world in a whole new way—and as such come into a new understanding of what life is actually about. The awakening process is quite interesting, and it often involves many different changes in a person's life. These include a change in their income level—often as a result of going into business on their own—as well as a change in their behavior. In many ways, spiritual awakening often entails much more than just seeing oneself as spiritually awakened—it is also about seeing how one fits into the greater universe—and that the universe itself has an inner spirit. As spiritual awakening is often so difficult to understand at first, it can also be quite an amazing thing—for many people. It is something that most people do not see in their entire lives, and for those who see it—they rarely live their lives as if they were spiritually awakened. As such, it is a process that most people do not even think about, and as such discover only after a significant time. This is why people who do become awakened often look back upon their lives and wonder what they were doing—and why they were doing it. In many ways, it is as if their life before awakening was a dream, and only after awakening did, they realize that there was more to what was going on—there was a divine spirit at play in their lives. As such, awakening can be quite difficult to adjust to—but well worth it.

Moving on to the Spiritual Awakening Triggers

This is a fairly recent area of research and writing in the field of spirituality and awakening. Exactly who are these triggers and exactly what they do is still unclear. Some people think they cause spiritual awakening, while others believe that if they did something would have to be done to stop them. The idea of "spiritual triggers" is fairly new and difficult to fully understand. A spiritual trigger is considered to be any external event that shakes a person's experience of reality, rendering their current belief system useless in dealing with the situation.

The people who are resistant to awakening are also resistant to spiritual triggers. This resistance leads them to feel as if they must be alone. They perceive their own resistance, and the resistance of others around them, as a sign that enlightenment is not possible for anyone else. This creates a sense of being stuck in a lower state, with no way out. One example of this controversy comes from a study done by Michael Murphy on the composition of spiritual awakenings. His research showed that nearly half of the participants in his study experienced significant religious decline or disintegration during their lifetime. He suggests that those who do not suffer decline are either born with a form of resistance and/or their beliefs have already been formed to such an extent, they do not need to be changed. As such, the two research directions, that of spiritual awakening triggers and decline/disintegration during a spiritual awakening, are not necessarily mutually exclusive.

Many people believe spiritual triggers are a known, and possibly inevitable part of the process of awakening. This is supported by the belief that without some kind of triggering event in life, one's idea of reality would be too rigid to change. People who feel this way often try to avoid discovering these triggers. This could mean staying in their current religious and spiritual group for as long as possible until a triggering event occurs. This is similar to the idea of the Downturn in Buddhism when people would refuse to accept new information.

Some people believe that spiritual awakening triggers are inevitable. This is due to a belief that there are no exceptions to what triggers become, such as how many times one may have been exposed to it before it triggers something. This belief is supported by the lack of any evidence that supports such an exception.

It should be noted that the idea of spiritual awakening triggers is fairly new and difficult to fully understand. The subject has been researched and written about by a variety of different writers and scientists.

Those who do experience spiritual awakening, typically learn so much more about their lives than they did before. They can see their lives as if they were unfolding in front of them—as opposed to in the future—and can adjust their behavior accordingly. As such, the experiences and insights gained from spiritual awakening can change a person's life as well.

Spiritual awakening is definitely a thing—but it can also be quite difficult to come to terms with. It is a process that most people do not see in their entire life, and they often only find out they are spiritually awakened after experiencing something amazing. Their outlook on life changes as well, and the experiences gained from spiritual awakening usually yield so much more in terms of knowledge.

After all, spiritual awakening can be very difficult to adjust to—and many people think of it as just another myth or fairy tale. Yet, for those who do experience it—they know that something is amazing going on. It is not simply that you are opening your soul—it is about finding out how much more meaningful life can be.

If you do happen to experience spiritual awakening, it is important to come to terms with what this means for your life—and how you should move forward as a result. After all, the experience of awakening often highlights the fact that there is more to life than meets the eye, or even that everything happens for a reason.

Chapter 8
Blockers for Spiritual Awakening

There are so many things that could be paralyzing you on your journey. From emotional struggles to physical ones or from going too fast to too slow, there are various ways to accidentally get in your own way, but this portion will help you at least open your eyes and realize what you can do to help.

Physical Challenges

The simple truth of the matter is that sometimes our bodies aren't ready for spiritual awakening quite yet. In some cases, it's due to an auto-immune disorder. Sometimes, it's caused by a lack of ability in a certain part of the body. Sometimes, still, it's caused by the inability to practice meditation due to extensive daily anxiety. Regardless of the physical challenges that are getting in your way, you are not a failure. You will come to a point in your healing when you will be able to handle spiritual awakening on top of everything else, but right now might not be that moment, and that's okay. Rushing one's kundalini awakening can be detrimental sometimes, and it's always best to just take it at a pace that feels natural and non-stressful for your experience and needs.

Experiencing Things With Too Much Intensity or Too Quickly

Sometimes, the chakras aren't that blocked, and they're relatively easy to open, cleanse, and align. For people that have this experience, the kundalini awakening process may happen much faster than it would for the standard, highly blocked individual. If this is the case for you, you'll likely have an incredibly intense experience right from the beginning, and it could even become too intense because of the speed of transition. If you're not rushing things and they're still advancing intensely and quicker than anticipated, try to meditate every other day. Try to take a step back in your process and allow it to become calmer, rescaled to anticipate what you can handle. You may also benefit immensely from having a guide or guru. Some people do not do well with these types of relationships in healing and awakening, but because you're so highly sensitive, a teacher or mentor—even just a listening supporter—may be just the thing.

Diet Doesn't Support Awakening

It may sound far-fetched to some (and I'd be willing to bet this "some" group of people is comprised mostly of meat-eaters), but sometimes, your diet will get in the way of your awakening. Saying that doesn't mean you need to go right ahead and cut out meat or dairy or gluten or sugar. It more so means that you may be able to aid your awakening process if you make a few slight adjustments. You can start by eating less processed food and more fruits and vegetables. If that's hard for you to do to start off, try beginning by eating one less meal with meat each week. Simply start small and see how you feel; see how your body reacts. If a positive response is evoked, make additional changes in accordance.

You're Focusing on the Wrong Body Part

Some issues with the spiritual awakening are rooted in the individual's abilities to focus, and these issues are easily adjusted with a switch of where one's attention goes when he or she meditates. For example, especially if you focus your energy on your head (or on your third eye) when you close your eyes to meditate (which most people do), you've found your problem right there. To instigate spiritual awakening, you need to start off by focusing your energy on your heart, belly, and gut. The kundalini needs a healthy environment to rise into, and if you're sending all that healthy attention to your third eye, you've skipped way beyond that gut space that the spiritual meets first.

Think of how the spirit will move and prepare your body accordingly. In essence, during your meditations, breathe deep into your stomach for a while and see what changes for you.

Your Mentality Ignores the Body or Vice Versa

It has to be balanced with physical efforts, as you're able to complete them. The connection with yoga is important here, for that practice can do a lot to aid in your kundalini's awakening. Mainly, kundalini yoga especially helps cleanse blockages in one's chakras through movement and body-focused breathing. In the same vein, one cannot instigate full kundalini awakening through just the practice of yoga. There has to be a balance between mind-based and body-based approaches in your overall attempt. Otherwise, you will continue on in this state of internal imbalance.

Poor or Unsupportive Mood

To a certain degree, kundalini awakening can help readjust mood and emotional imbalances, but one has to get to that point first. It could be that those heightened mood and emotional imbalances are what's keeping you from any clear direction in your hopes of awakening. Check your mindset! Check your most common moods! If there's any way you can begin to adjust those mindsets and moods, you're sure to see some difference in your kundalini practice in no time. It may sound complicated, pushy, or difficult now, but if you can somehow rise above any draining moods and emotions, you'll see your kundalini rise in kind.

Overwhelming Urges for Control

The purest kundalini awakenings indeed happen with absolutely no effort on behalf of the individual, but not all awakenings can happen like that. However, many distractions are blocking the divines that are everywhere these days. Ultimately, there should be no ego-based forcing, pushing, or controlling involved in one's awakening. But this whole book still helps its reader through techniques and tips to aid in his or her self-guided awakening, so it really just comes down to finding a balance. If you're struggling with the process, try to establish a better balance between self-guidance and trying to do too much too quickly, then see what happens.

Past Trauma or PTSD Is Too Strong of a Blockage

Sometimes, the traumas we bore witness to in the past (or that we're currently surviving) create blockages for us that become so entrenched and so ubiquitously spread throughout our chakras that we become unable to guide ourselves through our own awakenings. That's not a good or bad thing; it's simply a fact of life. If you feel that this sentiment applies to you, don't be put off from kundalini awakening, for there is incredible and life-altering hope for you. It just means that you might have to work through your traumas separately first. Based on what you've experienced, it may be supportive to talk to someone about that experience, whether it's a friend, partner, guardian (on this plane or another), or therapist. Use art therapy or music therapy if you'd rather not interact with another person, you'd rather not share your trauma with someone else, or you feel that you have no one else to share it with. Get that yuck out somehow! Try to be creative or communicative about it, and your kundalini will start rising in no time.

Unwillingness to Face One's True Nature

Awakening can be a tricky process at times. It's not always just positive signs and good feelings and happiness. Sometimes, you'll be made to face your flaws, and the task will be this: change them or suffer no further kundalini movement. It's a tough situation, but it definitely means that some people falter in the process of awakening because of these self-based reality checks. Furthermore, as the kundalini rises initially through the throat, third eye, and crown chakras (before it starts freely flow through all the open chakras), the individual will realize more and more how filled with divinity he or she is.

For some, this awareness is frightening or too much to handle. Some are simply unwilling to embrace this potential. To off-set from this situation if you find you're being held back similarly, what you can do is to practice radical openness and acceptance of yourself, divinity, and others.

No Community of Support

If you've ever heard someone, say that kundalini awakening will take your friends and family from you, you've probably just interacted with someone who tried to talk about his or her awakening with those closest to him or her, but the community couldn't or wouldn't support those efforts. This dismissal of awakening doesn't always happen, and even if it does happen to you concerning your close friends or family, don't let yourself get too down in the mouth quite yet! There are a few things you can do in this case:

1. Leave kundalini awakening out of it where these people are involved

2. As you continue on your awakening journey, your powers of attraction will be stronger than ever. With the right combination of hope and focus, you'll surely draw to you the right community of support in no time.

3. You can also keep trying with those friends and family, just with different tactics the next time.

4. You could even dismiss the idea of a supportive community entirely and build one yourself with information. There are a plethora of apps you can download that will help boost your awakening with supportive tips and advice, and for some people, this information switch is enough to make up for what people around them lack.

No Teacher or Guide

While some people will be self-guided in their awakenings with no issue, others do work much better toward that experience with a teacher or at least a mentor helping and guiding their paths. If you feel lost and are desperately seeking a teacher, my first recommendation is to seek out a yoga studio that teaches kundalini yoga. Strike up a conversation with the teacher there and see what blossoms from there. Alternatively, you could seek out kundalini chat rooms online, or if you prefer things in person, you could go to your local metaphysical store and ask around about meditation mentors. You never have to struggle alone. Let kundalini guide your confidence to enable you to draw in the people whose help you'll need for growth.

Environments Don't Support Awakening

Whether it's your home environment, your work environment, your economic environment, your natural environment, or otherwise, indeed, some spaces do not align with one's striving toward awakening. Sometimes, people talk trash, which can affect your flow. Sometimes, people might laugh at you for what you're passionate about. Other times, you might be surrounded by pollutants that keep, for example, your pineal gland calcified without your knowing. Trust your intuition here. If it feels like an unsafe place to meditate or do your yoga practice, try to find another space. If it feels like your well-being and sanity are threatened by being who you are and doing what you want to do, seek shelter elsewhere for this venture until you're strong enough to fight that vibe. You don't have to force this process, and you certainly don't have to do it where you're unable to feel safe.

Chapter 9
Spiritual Awakening and Anger

I know many people go through a spiritual awakening without any anger. I also know this is the exception and not the rule, because most of us have unresolved anger when we go through an awakening. For those who are curious about this, here's a bit of information that might be helpful to you. The truth is we were not meant to live life in a state of innocence. We were meant to live it with our full consciousness and awareness as spiritually awakened beings here on earth. We're in the gravity of consciousness that is much lower than we were meant to be. We have been betrayed by the spirit and our own egos, and so we have become trapped in the gravity of consciousness that is much lower than we were meant to be. As a result, we hold the anger of our past traumas. Our truth-telling requires us to see these past events clearly. It's not possible to truthfully tell our story if we deny them or distort them. Because our egos were raised in a lower gravity of consciousness, they automatically distrust anyone who can speak truth to them. They instinctively feel unjustly treated by those who speak their truth—and this triggers the fear response.

We have an instinctive tendency towards violence whenever we feel attacked, as a spiritual body that comes from our past traumas (or current attacks). We feel that the truth-teller wants to violate us, and this can result in aggression as we defend ourselves.

Truth-telling is a deep process of transformation towards the higher states of spirituality. To navigate this process, spiritual awakening must occur.

The important part of that journey is understanding our anger, guilt, and shame that arise out of our traumas and betrayal. Ignorance creates fear, and anger often comes out as self-defense in situations where we are being threatened. Being angry at the idea of speaking our truth is denying our past traumas, and so it is getting in the way of truth-telling. Those who are very angry when they start to speak their truth usually have unresolved anger from their past abuse. Ignorance is not an option for spiritual awakening, and so we must be willing to go through the process of discovery and transformation. Our ignorant resistance to truth-telling is very hard on our bodies, and this is why the physical body has a natural inflammation response when we experience anger.

Our egos are used to living in a place of ignorance, where they can avoid the truth at all costs. Our egos want to avoid being injured or killed when we speak our truth. This makes us vulnerable to becoming violent towards those who tell us the truth. We must learn to process our anger and transform ourselves to be able to truthfully tell our story. This includes dealing with any unresolved anger that arises from past traumas. Usually, this has been unconsciously denied in some way, so it must be consciously processed and healed.

When we allow this process of healing, we will be able to truthfully tell our story without triggering the out-of-body pain response in the physical body. All things are energy, and healing anger is a process of combining energy to heal traumas. This is a deep work of self-empowerment and transformation. We have a natural tendency to want to avoid pain, so we prefer to deny our traumas. This holds the pain in the body, which causes physical issues. The soul has no reason for being angry at anyone telling the truth. Sometimes the ego gets angry at the spirit, but we must see that these things are not true. Spirit has only our highest good in mind. No one who tells us our truth does so with malice or aggression in mind, but rather with a desire to free us of that which is holding us back—including anger at ourselves. We must step back from our egos as they are speaking and see that both of them are just parts of ourselves where awareness is blocked. We must be willing to see our own anger so we can heal it, and then step into our enlightened self. When we let go of our anger, we release a lot of energy that can then be directed into healing. This is a key component of spiritual awakening. If you are angry, you won't want to speak your truth freely. So, it becomes important to energetically heal the anger within ourselves, so that we can move freely towards our spiritual purpose. We are meant to live a life free from the fear of retaliation and violence. Once we can truthfully tell our story, and there is no fear of retaliation, we will be free to move towards healing ourselves. If you feel very angry when thinking about speaking your truth, this is a sign that you will benefit greatly from healing that anger. It's normal to feel these things when we are starting out in our spiritual path, but it's not normal to stay in that state for very long.

Healing our past traumas does not mean that we will forgive them. It points to the fact that we will be able to accept what happened and move on with our spiritual progression. We can feel disgusted, angry, or betrayed by someone who tells us the truth. But this is a normal reaction, so we must not get stuck in it. It's okay to feel angry or hurt when someone tells us our truth, but it's not okay to get stuck there. We must be willing to feel our anger and hurt to come out of that state. When we are stuck in that anger, it is keeping us from moving forward with our growth. If there's a way to free yourself from these feelings, do what you can. It's okay to feel angry at someone who tells us the truth, but it's important not to get wedged at that moment for long. It's normal to feel angry at someone who tells us the truth, but you must learn to let it go. Sometimes we feel angry at ourselves for getting upset by someone telling us our truth. It's important not to deny these feelings within us, but also to be willing to find a way out of the anger and hurt from the experience. It is not smart to get lodged in a place of anger or resentment towards any one person who tells us our truth. This will only hold us back from our own spiritual growth. If we feel anger towards a person, we must work through that as soon as possible. If someone tells us the truth, and we feel angry towards them for doing it, they are in a way helping us. It shows us what is blocking our energy, and consequently what needs to be healed for our higher selves to take charge of our lives.

When someone tells us the truth, it's normal for us to feel angry and hurt. We have to go through these feelings to move past them. If we suppress our feelings, they will only get worse. It is not wise to get stuck in a place of anger or resentment towards anyone who tells us our truth. If we feel anger towards a person, we must work through that as soon as possible. Sometimes we may feel angry at someone who tells us our truth, but it's important not to hold onto that anger for long. If we do, it only holds back our spiritual progress. We can choose how to respond to what they told us. It is not wise to keep the anger inside for long periods because it will only make things worse in the long run. We can choose not to talk about someone who tells us our truth, although at times this may be dangerous for ourselves and others. We can feel as though we have done the right thing in this situation, though. We just need to stay strong and keep our heads clear. We should not get angry when someone else is trying to tell us the truth. This is something that cannot be avoided if we are to progress spiritually, and it is important not to hold onto our anger for long periods. It can sometimes be helpful to tell someone else a lie about ourselves, even a little one. The lie is then said to be the truth to bring about a beneficial result. Even if we do not lie, it is human nature to have doubts about others. Only when we have no doubts can we remain strong and keep going. We are told that we should not tell the truth if it would cause trouble for others. This means that we shouldn't be honest about others, even if they ask for our truth. If someone asks us a question, which we know would upset them, we can look at them with compassion and say, 'I'm sorry I cannot tell you the truth.'" Every single person on earth has the right to know our true selves. This also includes the right to see how much trouble I/we are causing through dishonesty. If they've done this to us, it helps both of us move forward spiritually. If someone we care about is hurt by the truth that they demanded from us, then we hurt them equally by continuing to keep our true selves from them. If someone asks us to tell the truth, but we know it would cause them trouble, then we should not give it to them. But if we do tell them anyway, they are being selfish and expecting too much from us. This puts our relationship under stress and so it isn't helpful for anyone.

Chapter 10
Spiritual Awakening and Anxiety

You will inevitably question your beliefs, and this may lead to feelings of angst and anxiety. These feelings are often a symptom of a spiritual crisis, which is often accompanied by feelings of disorientation and alienation. When you find yourself in this place, it's important to understand that these emotions are temporary. Trust your thoughts, follow your heart, and allow time for you to heal.

There are many causes for this but I have found that the greatest two may be the trouble of the unknown and fear of losing control. At this time, you will find it helpful to remember that you are on a spiritual path, not an emotional one. You don't need to speed through these emotions when they arise. Allow yourself to sit with them while you embrace your higher consciousness, and work through them slowly and deliberately. As always, remember that you do not have to go through this alone. Reach out to someone you trust, practice self-compassion, and choose to stay open and flexible. This will ultimately help you on your journey. You are not alone through this time as many other souls feel the same way as you do, but many have difficulty accessing their intuition due to trauma or social conditioning.

We have written about how important it is to not let anxieties get the better of you. You must comprehend how to manage your fears to avoid them from running your life. The first aspect to acknowledge is that your feelings of fear and anxiety are not real. Your brain is simply making associations about the world around you, and your body knows this to be true. You can actually work with these emotions if you choose, especially if you practice mindfulness. The greatest fear of all is the unknown. We have no notion of what the future has for us, but we often obsess over it anyway. This is because we feel uncomfortable with where our life is going at this moment, as though there's more to come in the future, and we want to know what it will be. The unknown represents a new opportunity and fresh air, yet it also represents a lack of security for many people. Anxiety can create a sense of unease over our collective future; a sense that we don't know what's coming around the corner. Or, that we don't know who we are or what we're about. This is an expression of the fear of change and unknowns, which can tend to cause people to fret over life to excess. The anxiety caused by these anxieties can easily overwhelm you daily. When this happens, it's often helpful to know that there is a way out. The medium to having a productive and meaningful life, especially when anxiety strikes are by learning to meditate for anxiety. Based on scientific evidence, meditation is used to help individuals stay calm and relaxed in the face of stressful conditions. By knowing this, you are able to let go of some of your anxieties because you know how to deal with them. The root of anxiety is the fear of change—the fear that we do not fully possess the ability to control the flow of events in our lives. But, by using several techniques, you can manage your anxiety and develop a healthier relationship with it. One such method is meditation or mindfulness, which allows you to let go of your anxieties and reduce your overall symptoms. There are numerous mediums that you can use to cast away your anxieties.

Learning to Meditate for Anxiety

To begin with, you can learn to meditate using one of many guided meditation techniques available on the internet. By listening to these guided meditations, you can gain a greater understanding of what is involved in mindfulness and how it can help to manage anxiety. There are many different styles of meditation, including transcendental meditation and mindfulness meditation; all of which have been proven highly successful in managing anxiety and reducing symptoms. Regardless of which meditation method you use, the important thing is to keep practicing and keep pushing forward.

Reach Out

Anxiety is sometimes caused by a major life event. For example, if you have recently been diagnosed with cancer and haven't told your loved ones yet, or if you've just been dumped by your spouse, this can cause anxiety to run rampant in your life. It may be difficult to grasp where to go for help when anxiety is triggered by events in your life. This is why it's important to reach out and talk on the phone with someone.

Not only will you find that your worries subside, but you'll also have a friend to turn to when you're down and out.

Talk to Someone

Talking to someone about what has been going through your mind can be beneficial for many people.

Not only will you find that you feel better after you open up, but you may also feel a bit of relief after your mind is off of the event. Whether or not the event was a one-time thing or something that has been going on for a prolonged time, talking about it can help to ease anxiety.

Meditate

By taking some time out of your day to meditate, you'll apparently be able to relax yourself and reduce anxiety symptoms. Meditating has been shown to reduce overall anxiety levels and even help to deal with panic attacks.

Three minutes a day of meditation can be beneficial, and the great part about it is that you can do it anywhere. As a result, there's no excuse not to meditate.

Exercise

Exercising works in two different ways when it comes to managing anxiety symptoms. First off, exercise provides people with an outlet in which they can release pent-up energy and stress. Doing something that gets your heart racing, such as running or playing tennis, tends to help people to cope with stress and anxiety healthily. Secondly, exercise has also been shown to elevate serotonin levels in your brain. And we all recognize how critical serotonin is when it comes to dealing with anxiety and depression.

Do Something You Love

Finding an activity that you enjoy doing is crucial when it comes to decreasing anxiety levels because this will allow you to relax and reduce stress. If you find something that you love doing, then you will most likely look forward to the activity and make time to do it. If you find yourself dreading a particular activity, then it might be best to avoid it altogether.

Laugh Often

Finding humor in life's struggles can go a long way towards helping to reduce anxiety. This is why so many people rely on comedy shows such as "The Daily Show with Jon Stewart" or "The Colbert Report" for relief from the problems in their everyday lives. I highly recommend that you do this by using affirmations. One of the most helpful tools to help with anxiety is keywords or phrases that will help make you feel safe, like this one: "The Universe loves me." Let this phrase sink deeply into your subconscious mind so that it can work for you on a gut level. Another great affirmation to use is "this or something better" as it will help to remind you that there are no bad situations, only different paths. These might not seem like they could work, but most people who repeat these phrases find themselves feeling better in no time at all. In addition to using affirmations, I also recommend taking up meditation. This will help you to still your mind and relax any nervousness that gets in the way of your intuition. When it comes to anxiety, I highly recommend that you try acupuncture and Chinese herbal medicine. Acupuncture is one of the most effective natural treatments for anxiety disorders when properly used, and although there are many schools of thought about this, it is important to use a practitioner that is trained in acupuncture, as opposed to just researching on Wikipedia. In addition to acupuncture, I also suggest trying various herbs such as St. John's Wort, Valerian Root, and Bach Flower Remedies. These herbs can be used for anxiety or they can be taken on an empty stomach to help with sleep. In fact, you must get enough sleep to help calm any anxiety or restless mind you may have. A lot of people have worries about herbal medicine, but these remedies are very safe as long as you use them correctly. There are other helpful herbs such as chamomile if you would prefer to go that route.

When it comes to nutrition, the first thing you need to do is start eating a diet that is full of whole, plant-based foods. A lot of people begin a "cleanse" or "detox" to cure their anxiety, but this is the wrong approach. Instead, you should try to eat a healthy diet full of fruits, vegetables, and whole grains. I recommend that you focus on eating a lot of dark leafy greens such as spinach and kale as they are very rich in vitamins and minerals.

Most people find that they feel better when they decrease their intake of animal products. In fact, I would recommend going vegan if you can at least try for one month.

Chapter 11
The After-Effects of Awakening

When a spiritual awakening occurs, it awakens our consciousness to our own feelings. That is how it all begins. We regain the ability to analyze our internal operations. Spiritual awakening can arrive in a few forms. It typically comes in a variation of some stages:

Unhappiness and Feeling Empty

This could stem from something terrible that has happened in your life. Sometimes you may not even know precisely what is causing the depression or confusion. This typically comes about during a life crisis or out of a natural state, such as a divorce, trauma, death, illness, or a life-changing event. Regardless of how it has come about, you may find yourself isolated from the rest of the world, which will not help you at all.

Change in Perspective

In this stage, you may wake up a bit, and you will start to recognize the lies that have occurred around you. You will still be unhappy and will get into a feeling of disgust with what is going on around you. In this stage, you will be angry at times and then sad—it may seem as you are on a roller coaster of emotions. That is your mind working. The stages are something many go through before they have a spiritual awakening. Some may recognize when that occurs; however, some may not. Here are some signs of spiritual awakening.

You Avoid Negative People

If someone is gossiping, judging, and engaging in other dramatic behavior, you tend to avoid those people. You get to a point where you will find that petty.

You Have Increased Intuition

You tend to focus on others' actions more so than listening to what they are saying. Actions do speak louder than words. Just make sure you are watching, and never take anyone's word over what you have observed. Manipulative people will try to alter the situation.

You Have Increased Inner Peace

You do not need validation. You will crave quiet time and alone time more often. Social media will start to take a back seat in your life. You will find that you do not need to post on social media to see how many likes you get; you will feel content in your own body. Spiritual awakening can be a fantastic experience when you receive it. A spiritual awakening can cause someone to transform their life, happiness, health, and abundance at a speedy rate. This class of circumstance is not always easy to handle; however, when a spiritual awakening does happen, it will make your life better permanently. Once you get through the ups and downs, you will see how amazing the experience can be, and you will never want to lose it. For many people, spiritual awakening is a complicated and confusing process to understand. This can make it difficult for people to know what this phenomenon means for them. The experience of spiritual awakening is personal, and it varies from person to person. It may be something as small as a few tears when watching a movie, or if an encounter with nature helps you feel alive again. Different types of awakenings may last the course of days, weeks, or even decades. This can make the experience of spiritual awakening hard to understand, since people may think that it is a single experience that only lasts for a short time. The following will explore the different energies associated with spiritual awakening and how they can affect you. The most common kind of spiritual awakening is when you feel heightened chakras. You may feel happy and positive as if you are walking on air. People often describe this feeling as feeling alive again or coming alive for the first time. This kind of awakening is rather transitory, and people tend to feel it at the beginning. It means that you are starting to get in touch with who you really are and discover your true self. Another kind of awakening that people experience is when they start to understand more about the spiritual world and how it works. Instead of feeling happy, they may begin to feel more fascinated by this new knowledge, especially by their own psychic abilities. They may feel excited and encouraged about their place in the spiritual community. They may feel that they have a mission to fulfill, and they are eager to bask in the glory that comes with this mission. They may feel as if they have been awakened to some great Truth that will bestow on them eternal happiness. Another kind of spiritual awakening is when people experience psychic abilities for the first time or increase their powers. This usually comes later, after someone has had time to become familiar with the spirit realm and cultivate his or her abilities. During this awakening, people are usually able to do things that they couldn't do before, such as foresee the future or read other people's emotions. They may also be able to hear or see things that aren't really real. However, they may begin to feel confused and unsure of their abilities, when they realize that they may be reaching for powers that are beyond them.

People who decide to practice meditation or spirituality often experience these kinds of awakenings. This may be the most common kind of awakening since it is what people usually do to get in touch with their spirituality. They may feel confused and exhilarated by their own psychic abilities. They may feel overwhelmed by their visions or dreams, but they also see it as an opportunity to grow spiritually and understand themselves better. However, some people who are interested in spirituality and meditation may experience the opposite effects. They typically feel calm and peaceful for the first few days or weeks, after which they become restless or uncomfortable. During this time, they feel that their lives are more purposeful or meaningful, but then all of the sudden the experience disappears and no longer feels like a spiritual awakening. The experience of spiritual awakening may be very positive for some people. They may find it exciting to feel as if they are experiencing some great Truth and that they are doing something with their lives. They may feel an intense sense of purpose in life, and they become more motivated to face the challenges ahead. However, for others, spiritual awakening can be a tumultuous experience. They may be afraid of losing control over their lives or losing sight of their goals in life. Instead of feeling as if they are becoming more self-aware, they may be more confused and unsure of themselves.

Many people who experience spiritual awakenings at a certain age find that it is never the same again. This change in energy can make it rather difficult to understand what the experience exactly means for them. For those who have experienced a spiritual awakening, they may notice that this energy is very different from the rest of their life. They may feel that this is the first time that they have been truly alive and are experiencing the fullness of life. They may also realize that they are on a journey, and there are still many things to be accomplished. However, for others, this process can take place over years or even over decades. There may be some people who believe that this experience is an ending and doesn't really exist anymore. However, for others, this is just the beginning of something much greater. Many factors affect your spiritual awakening. Your life experiences and developmental history undoubtedly play a role in this process. Many people begin to practice meditation or spirituality when they are feeling stuck in life or unfulfilled by their lives. They typically begin with practices such as yoga or meditation and realize their connection with energy and universal energy at the beginning of this process. As they continue to meditate and develop their abilities, they will gain a deeper understanding of themselves and how the spiritual world works. At this point, they may be attracted to spiritual teachings or teachings that explain how the spirit realm works. They may want to have a more powerful experience with spirituality so that they can understand the connections between the physical world and the spiritual world. However, they can also progress in the opposite direction. They may begin to feel uncomfortable with meditation or spirituality and realize that their lives need to be more grounded and have more meaning. At this point, they may focus on a particular goal in life, such as finding a job or getting married, or raising a family. The type of experiences that you have while going through your spiritual awakening will affect this process.

Chapter 12
Pros and Cons of Spiritual Awakening

Pros

Many people wonder what the advantages of a spiritual awakening are because they're not certain if they can benefit from it. It's good to know that this kind of spiritual awakening is beneficial in all aspects of life, though, as it gives you a deeper appreciation for who you are and how your actions affect those around you. What's more, many believe that it helps with your physical health in the long run. Here are just a few of the advantages of a spiritual awakening.

You'll have an Overall Better Understanding of Yourself

We all go through life living with certain expectations about who we are and what our place in the world is. But if you go through a spiritual awakening, you start to discover that your former expectations don't necessarily reflect reality and that they may even be standing in the former of your happiness. In a spiritual awakening, you'll learn that you're greater than you think and that your potential is truly limitless.

It Will Boost Your Self-Confidence

Self-doubt can hold us back from achieving success in many areas of life, but when we believe in ourselves, we become unstoppable. Those who go through a spiritual awakening come to have more faith in themselves and their own potential. This newfound self-confidence helps them to feel good about themselves and to accomplish the things they put their mind to.

You'll Discover That You're a Part of Something Bigger

We each come into this world alone and leave it alone, but there's a big part of life in between those two moments that we can experience only as part of a family, community, or another group. If you go through a spiritual awakening, you'll learn that your actions can impact many more people than you realize and that it's important to think about how they affect others before taking any action.

It Will Help You to Appreciate Life

The world is one big playground, and it's easy to forget that when we get involved in every little drama. But during a spiritual awakening, you can experience a new and deeper appreciation for how amazing the world really is, and how lucky you are to be able to live in it. This newly found appreciation will help you to feel more grateful for the time you have here on earth.

It Will Make Your Life Easier

We all encounter difficulties at different points in our lives and it's easy to get frustrated with them when we don't know how to deal with them. But if you go through a spiritual awakening, you'll learn that facing challenges can actually help you to grow and become wiser and that they're not really as scary as you might have thought before. When you realize this, your fear will lessen and obstacles will lose much of their power over your life.

It Will Help You Be More Compassionate

Along with your appreciation of the world will come to a greater compassion for those around you, as well as an awareness of how their actions affect you and others. Being aware of this will help you to start being more patient and understanding, which in turn makes life easier for the people around you.

It Will Give You More Motivation to Act

In a world where people often fail to see the importance of what they're passionate about, it can be hard to see the value in anything you do. But when you go through a spiritual awakening, you'll start to realize that love, like all things, is something that has real value and that should be given now and then. That's when you'll start focusing on the things that truly make you happy.

It Can Help You Maintain Your Sanity During Tough Times

When we're going through a hard time it can be hard to maintain our composure, but spiritual awakenings can help us to keep our wits about us. They can provide a sense of calm and peace that helps us to stay upbeat throughout the ordeal.

It Will Bring You Closer to Others

The world is full of people who are suffering and feel alone, which makes it important for you to reach out to those around you during your own tough times. But as you go through a spiritual awakening, you'll see that the people in your life are part of a bigger family, and thus they become more important to you.

It Can Cause Your Faith to Grow

When we're down and out, our faith can flag because our lives get harder and we struggle with doubts about why our fate is so tough. But when you go through a spiritual awakening, your faith can grow stronger, because you start to realize that all of this is part of a plan by God and that there's an answer for everything in life.

It Can Help You Live a Healthier Lifestyle

Many people turn to food when they're unhappy with their life or they feel stressed out and anxious, either by themselves or others. But if you go through a spiritual awakening, you'll begin to understand that the source of your happiness is within, and thus there's no reason to deny yourself those feelings by using food as a crutch.

It Will Help You Appreciate the Present

Life is one big gift, but it's easy to forget this when we're busy wishing for things to be different from what they are. But as you go through a spiritual awakening, you'll see that the present moment is one of the best things that can happen to you and that everything in it is full of wonder and potential.

Cons

Spiritual awakening is an experience, sometimes sudden and dramatic and sometimes a gradual process of realization that happens when one has a direct experience of the Divine. It's very different from religious conversion or being "born again" in that it may not be related to any specific religious ideas for a person. Let us explore the disadvantages of having an awakening experience. What are the pitfalls of spiritual awakening?

They May Feel Incredible Guilt for What They Have Done to Create the Opportunity for Their Spiritual Advancement

For example, one may have harmed another person to have them open up and experience their own higher purpose. One may use guilt to make another person a better person while feeling guilty for having taken this action. When a person is enlightened, they have no more needs guilt as this negative emotion is no longer useful to them as they already have become a better person. Their past actions no longer bother them as they have transcended the need for guilt. While this can be liberating at first, the person may realize that guilt was the tool that they used to become who they are and without it, there is no way to truly experience and understand who they are or what their higher purpose is.

One Feels Unfulfilled to Know Others Are Going Through What They Just Experienced Without Having Any Idea What It Really Is

This lack of fulfillment will make the person yearn for higher meaning, and this can cause them to start creating stories and myths around their awakening to fill this emptiness, or they may get attracted to spirituality like a moth to a light bulb.

The Person Now Has No Attachment to Their Former Identity

Thus becomes too attached to himself self and begins to really get into the idea of living a spiritual lifestyle like a monk in a monastery. This can be especially detrimental for people who may have been religious because they now have no idea what that was about. When one is awakened, it can be hard to find a balance between the way that they were before their awakening and the way they now exist.

The Person Becomes Obsessed with the Idea of How Great They Are and How Enlightened They Are

This can create an obsession to be kept up with to keep up with the feeling. This is a kind of OCD and can lead to more problems in one's life than it resolves. When a person has reached awakening, they should not just sit there and feel good about their experience. They need to understand what this experience was all about so that they can continue living on their higher path without needing anything else.

The Person May Think That He/She is Better Than Others Around him/her

This is a very common outcome of awakening, and not just because of the need for self-validation but also because someone who has experienced something so profound will naturally become eager to share it with others, even if the others are in no way interested. They will want to share this experience, as it is, in their own way.

The Person Becomes Over-Excited By the Fact of Having Had an Awakening Experience and Thinks They Are Some Kinds of "Super Human"

They think they are on a higher level of realization than others when in reality there is no such thing. The ego can take control and cause the person to think they are better than others in this way. This is not a true realization, but rather a feeling of superiority.

The Person Becomes Too Attached to Their Experience

They have become attached to it because they do not understand what it really means to be spiritually awakened, nor do they understand how much work this entails to keep up with their newfound understanding of self. As the person tries to keep up with this new understanding and understanding that others are not in the same place you will notice they become more demanding, critical, and negative instead of being humble.

The Person May Become Too Attached to Their Higher Purpose or Enlightenment and Create a Separation from Their Family and Friends

This has terrible potential. When you become too attached to your higher purpose you find that this is all there is to life and that everything else is an obstacle to your higher purpose. Because your experience of awakening has caused a separation from other people, this can create a vacuum in one's life and cause loneliness.

Chapter 13
How to Remove Negativity and Clean Aura

When lots of people hear about the phrase negative influence, they assume it has to do with drugs, alcohol, or other social vices. However, the phrase negative influence is more than social vices. Negative influence implies those bad influences that push you into making bad decisions. For example, you can be influenced into thinking bad about yourself. This will lead to low self-esteem. You can also be affected to think a negative thought about your life or your job. This could lead to suicide if not curtailed fast. Negative influence doesn't stop at having negative thoughts or suggestions; it can lead to negative habits as well. Getting rid of removing negative influence can be a daunting challenge. Your task of removing negative influence can be made more difficult if people with negative habits surround you. Furthermore, these individuals will remind you of your negative habits and will be forced to indulge in them even when you are trying to remove them. However, all hope is not lost. All you need is commitment and perseverance, and you will be able to remove negative influence, turn things around and begin to leave your life with more positivity. The first step to take if you want to remove negative influence is to change the people you spend time with. The next thing is to adjust the way you spend your time. These changes will help you find peace and joy in your life. What you must know is that the greatest negative influence you have is associating with negative people. They are pessimists and will use this pessimism to demoralize you. They waste your time on unimportant tasks and criticize you to the core if you are not in line with them. Negative people destroy you gradually till you are completely damaged. By being damaged, you result in alcohol, drugs, cigarettes, etc. When they notice you have become worthless, they abandon you. The very first step you should take in removing negative people is by identifying them. Where do you see negative people? Are they in your school, workplace, etc.? Recognizing a problem is the first step to solving it. As an individual who wants to get rid of negative influences, you need to identify the negative people around you. This may include negative people you associate within the office, school if you are a student, or at home if you are not living alone. To help you identify these individuals, look at the role of your friends in your life. Do you have friends at work or home who make you late for work, squander your time on frivolous activities? They can also make you feel bad about your achievements and growth. These are negative influences, and if you have such friends, it is time to make new ones.   As a student, if you have friends in school who regularly give you negative vibes by making negative comments about feeling alone or make you feel sad with their comments such as 'you're not unique,' 'you're not intelligent.' If you want to remove negative influences in your life, you need to stay away from these people. Make new friends who will make you feel good about yourself. The next place you should look at to identify negative influence is in your home, assuming you don't stay alone. It possible to have family members or roommates who influence you negatively. To recognize their role at home, look out for family members who make you question who you are and your identity. Look out for statements like 'you are so dumb, when are you going to grow up?' people who make such statements about you or to you at home are a negative influence on your life. This is because they make you feel resentful towards your life. They create doubt in your mind about who you really are. They also destroy your self-esteem gradually until you begin to feel worthless.

How to Handle Negative Influences

Having identified those who bring negative influence into your life, the next logical question you should ask yourself is " How do I handle these individuals that influence me negatively?" We have highlighted some steps below to help you handle negative influences.

Spend Less Time with Negative Individuals

As soon as you successfully identify negative people in your life, you should take steps to avoid them. It doesn't matter where the negative person is. Put some distance between you and them. This will give time to think about yourself and rediscover yourself without them being around to distract you. You can distance yourself from negative people by reducing the amount of time you spend on the phone with them if they are a bit far from you. You can also avoid having a one-on-one conversation with them. Have positive friends around you when you want to talk to them so they can see what positive thinking all is about. When you want to go out shopping or maybe dinner, rather than being alone with your cynical friend, invite other friends to join you guys. This will stop you from being left alone with your cynical friend. You are in control of your time. No one else is. Don't allow a negative person to dictate how you spend your time. They are energy drainers. A time that is wasted is a time that can't be recovered. So, spend your time wisely. They will never contribute anything meaningful to your life, other than push you to join them in whining away your precious time. Don't allow negative people to waste your time.

Build Boundaries Between You and the Source of Your Negative Influence

To remove negative influence on your life, set boundaries between you and the source of the negative influence. Building boundaries will make you feel safe and in control around a negative influence. While setting up boundaries may be useful in handling certain individuals, you may discover that some will try to infringe on these boundaries. Try to maintain your limits as much as possible even when you feel you have encroached on them. Building boundaries to keep out negative influence is essential, especially when your negative influence is the type you can't cut off completely. To avoid being contagious, keep anything that could influence you negatively and that includes negative people. You must keep them at arm's length. When in a group hangout, learn to be concise and talk less. Being wordy with details will only exploit you and you could end up talking about the things you aren't meant to talk about.

Display a Positive Attitude with a Negative Person

However, to handle or diffuse their negativity, you should show them a positive response when they show their negative attitude. Recover your positive attitude by balancing out their negative displays with your positive ones.

Stop Negative Talk/Thought About Yourself

Negative self-talk is as damaging as negative habits. You can engage in negative talk but only focusing on the bad things happening in your life rather than the good ones. Negative talk can also apply to the way you think about yourself. For example, a night of hangout may be canceled by your pals. Rather than letting it go, you begin to tell yourself that it was canceled because of you. You use words like 'no one likes me that is why they don't want to hang out with me. Another example can be something like this. After having a very productive day at work, you come home rather than being happy about your day; you begin to tell yourself how much work you couldn't get done.

Turn Negative Talk to Positive Ones

If you want to remove negative influence, you need to turn negative talk about yourself into positive ones. The power of the mind is crucial to the way you see yourself. Negative thoughts lead to negative speech, and negative talk leads to negative influence. You can change all that but having positive thoughts about yourself and, in turn, have a positive talk about yourself.

Start by evaluating any negative thought that comes into your mind. After evaluation, give a positive response to that particular negative thought. Make use of positive responses.

Be Yourself

It's easy to impress someone or look good for someone, but it's not always wise. The simple fact is you can't always satisfy everyone. Instead of making yourself look good for others, why not focus on making yourself happy? Don't impress anyone, let alone a negative person. Be yourself and spend quality time trying to figure out the things that make you happy. Spend time with people that will accept who you are and what you stand for. Don't pursue the wrong thing.

Determine Your Attitude

A person associating with a negative person does so at his/her own peril. They are toxic and introduce toxicity into your life. You don't have the willpower to make your own decisions because you are surrounded by pessimists. Don't allow negative people to dictate how you should respond or how your mood should be. You are yourself and in control of whatever that's happening to you. Choose how you want to behave. Choose how you want to be. Decide how you run your life because it's yours and no one else's.

Reduce Negative Habits

You can't get rid of or remove negative influences if you don't remove negative habits first. These negative habits, like smoking, heavy drinking, and regular partying, could make you feel good momentarily, but they have a lasting negative impact on your dreams and aspirations. They generally leave you with a wicked hangover and a negative feeling in the morning. This negative feeling in the morning will cause time mismanagement. Time mismanagement means that you won't have enough time during the day to pursue your dreams and engage in those activities that will facilitate your career development. Stopping all your negative habits will be a good way to handle negative influences in your life. Still, from experience, I know it will be difficult to stop all bad habits suddenly, so I suggest cutting back on your negative habits. This will go a long way to removing negative influences in your life. For example, rather than go out every night after work to the bar for a couple of drinks that usually lead to one too many, cut it back to once or twice a week.

Have a Positive Lifestyle

You can get rid of negative influences by leaving a positive lifestyle. You can start by having healthy meals. Healthy meals should include a large portion of self-made meals and less junk. A balanced diet of protein, vegetables, and fruits, as well as milk, should be part of your meals. Remember to drink adequate water as well to stay hydrated. Cut down a soda or possibly avoid it completely as well as other sugary drinks. The next part of your positive lifestyle should be to get sufficient sleep. This is one thing most people don't pay much attention to but, a sufficient amount of sleep every day plays a role in your mood and how you feel about yourself.

Chapter 14
How to Balance Your Chakras

As long as we're balancing the rest of your life, we might as well balance your chakras as well. When they are in balance, you will experience a heightened level of mental, emotional, and spiritual harmony. This ritual will bring you into that harmonious state by taking you through each of the chakras from root to crown, opening and balancing each in turn. It is based on visualization, affirmation, and meditation.

Balancing Your Root Chakra

The Root Chakra is your connection to the physical world, the earth we live on, and everything associated with our bodily requirements. You can tell that the Root Chakra is unbalanced by odd feelings of peril disconnection from the world. To balance the Root Chakra, visualize a red light filling up the Root Chakra and radiating out and down into the Earth. You will ground and connect yourself with the Earth and the world around you by doing this. Now, as you visualize this red light, as you feel its heat, meditate upon a grounding affirmation. You can make up one of your own, one that makes you feel especially grounded, or you can try one of the following:

- My roots are strong, my roots are deep.
- I stand firm as an oak.
- I am trustworthy.
- I am safe.

Balancing Your Sacral Chakra

The Sacral Chakra is the main point of your sexuality as well as interpersonal pleasures. If it is out of balance, your sexuality, as well as the ability to commit and to enjoy things, are blocked, as is your ability to properly care for yourself. To balance the Sacral Chakra, place your right hand over your abdomen, just below the navel, and imagine it stuffing it up with orange light. Feel the warmth of the light radiating through your body, mingling with the red light of the Root Chakra. As you do so, meditate upon an affirmation that honors the Sacral Chakra and all that it does. Again, you can make up one of your own, or use one of the following:

- I am a potent and creative being.
- I am sexually powerful.
- I know my needs and meet them.

Balancing Your Solar Plexus Chakra

Your Solar Plexus Chakra is the main point of your identity, your strength, and your life force. You will know that it is out of balance when you feel powerless, fearful of rejection, and find your self-esteem being eroded as your inner critic whispers its judgments and criticisms. To balance the Solar Plexus Chakra, visualize a powerful yellow light filling up your insides between the chest and naval. See it mingle with the lights of the Root and Sacral chakras and feel the growing heat and the flow of energy between them. Let the power of the Solar Plexus Chakra fill you as you meditate upon an affirmation that focuses on life, strength, and your own identity. Make a unique version of your own making, or try one of these:

- I am brave and powerful.
- I am enough.
- I love myself.

Balancing Your Heart Chakra

Your Heart Chakra is, of course, the center for matters of the heart and emotions in general. When it is out of balance, your feelings and views on love and emotion are skewed with bitterness and anger, loneliness, jealousy. It can unfortunately also turn the other way with obsession, desperation, neediness, and worries about being left. To balance your Heart Chakra, place the palm of your right hand over your heart and inhale deeply, visualizing a deep, glowing emerald, green light filling your chest with each breath. See it mingle with the light and energy of the Root, Sacral, and Solar Plexus chakras and feel the energy course through you. As you do this meditate upon an affirmation related to the Heart Chakra, one of your own or one of these:

- I am worthy of forgiveness and I forgive myself.
- I am worthy of love and I love myself.
- I am desirable.

Balancing Your Throat Chakra

As you know, the Throat Chakra governs communication, expression, and creativity. When it is out of balance, communication becomes difficult. You feel as though you cannot speak your mind that you are not allowed to express your opinions. You will also find that creative outlets, such as writing, or drawing are blocked. To balance the Throat Chakra, place your dominant hand on your throat, fingers loosely curled around the side of your neck, the palm centered on the throat. Now, visualize, as before, the Throat Chakra filling with an effulgence of sapphire blue light. Again, as before, feel the energy combine with the chakras below, feel it flow through you, warming you, energizing you.

- My words are clear.
- My meaning is clear.
- What I have to say is important
- I have wisdom and experience to share.

Balancing Your Third Eye Chakra

The Third Eye Chakra, as tackled, is the seat of your inner wisdom as well as your psychic and intuitive abilities, so when it is blocked, you would naturally feel cut off from those things, unable to connect with them and their ability to help you through life. As a result, your ability to learn important life and spiritual lessons, as well as to assess the things that frighten you, will be compromised. Finally, if your Third Eye Chakra is out of balance, it can make connecting with your Crown Chakra that much more difficult. Balancing the Third Eye Chakra begins with visualizing a powerful indigo light glowing just between and slightly above your eyebrows, the location of the Third Eye Chakra. Let this light, as before, fill your head and then mingle with the light and energy coming from the lower chakras.

- I value new ideas and concepts.
- I am guided by truth and goodness.
- I am a fountain of wisdom and intuition.

Balancing Your Crown Chakra

Your Crown Chakra connects you to the world of Spirit. When it is out of balance, you will feel far too connected with the physical world and somehow isolated away from the spiritual world. You may not notice at first, but before long you will feel something is missing, a kind of spiritual lack that can be fixed only by rebalancing your Crown Chakra.

To balance your Crown Chakra, visualize a blinding white light, as bright and as powerful as a spotlight, coming down from above and filling your Crown Chakra with incredible spiritual energy. Let that energy flow down through your Third Eye, Throat, Heart, Solar Plexus, Sacral, and Root chakras As it flows within you, feel the energy reach every part of your body. See it flow down through you into the Earth and circulate back up again, making you the connection between the realm of the spirit and the realm of the physical.

While you are visualizing all of this, meditate on affirmations that honor your connection with the universe and the divine. You can make up one of your own, something special that speaks to your personal connection with the universe, or you can try one of these:

- I am a vessel of divinity.
- I am part of a wider universe.
- My spirit is powerful.
- I am guided by divine wisdom.
- I am in the universe and the universe is in me.
- I cherish all life.
- I can hear the divine

Maintain this practice at least twice a week, more if you can, until you can do it easily. When you can, you will have a powerful tool that you can call upon at any time to open and empower your chakras and get your spiritual energy flowing through your body.

Nourishing Your Chakras

Energy work to open and balance your chakras is important, and you need to dedicate yourself to practicing these techniques, but there is something else you need to consider. Your body needs nourishment and given the connection between your physical and subtle forms; it makes sense that your diet needs to include foods that will nourish your chakras. By taking this approach, you will see your chakra health and wellbeing increase, thereby increasing your overall health and wellbeing. So, let's take a look at some of these important foods.

Feeding the Root Chakra

The Root Chakra grounds and connects you to the earth around you, so it makes sense that foods connected with roots and grounding would be appropriate for this chakra, so what could be better than root vegetables? Whether you eat them roasted, baked, in a soup, or even raw, they offer valuable nutrients to your physical body, great taste to please your palette, and an abundance of grounding energy. Add some red meat to the dish, and red fruit for dessert, all of which are very grounding and good for the Root Chakra, and you'll have a delicious meal that will keep your roots strong and solidly connected with the Earth.

Feeding the Sacral Chakra

The Sacral Chakra is associated with the element of water, so clear, cool water, tea, juices, clear broths, soups, and other liquids are appropriate. Water is best, followed by orange juices, but pretty much any liquid will do. As far as solid foods go, Sweet, juicy fruit and orange-colored foods like carrots—a root vegetable that will also help your Root Chakra—will all help to keep your Sacral Chakra strong.

Feeding the Solar Plexus Chakra

Since this is the seat of your power, where potential becomes power, bright yellow foods reminiscent of the Sun, especially if they have a little spice or sweetness to them, will help to keep this chakra in fighting trim. Yellow peppers and curries, bananas, corn, and other yellow foods. Even yellow tortillas will help. Just make sure the food you choose is the sort that doesn't digest quickly, whole grains, complex carbs, and nothing processed.

Feeding the Heart Chakra

The Heart Chakra is the point of balance between the lower and upper chakras, the transition between the physical and the spiritual chakras. It's also associated with the color green. Because of these qualities, the best foods for the Heart Chakra are green vegetables, leafy or cruciferous, which match the color of the chakra and, according to traditional Chinese medicine, are perfectly balanced between yin and yang.

Feeding the Throat Chakra

The color for the Throat Chakra is blue, and it is healed and energized by truth and speech. Nourishment for this chakra is found in foods with blue colors and tree-grown fruits. Blueberries, plums, and also peaches and apples, pears, and apricots. They are believed to know just the right moment to drop from their tree, ripe and ready to eat. In so doing, they communicate their own truth.

Feeding the Third Eye and the Crown Chakras

Given the almost entirely spiritual nature of the Third Eye and Crown Chakras, there really isn't much in the way of earthly food that will nourish them. Rather, they draw energy from divinity, love, and the spiritual realm. Because of this etheric nature, what you eat should not be grounding or heavy. Light meals are suitable when you are working with these chakras.

Chapter 15
Kundalini Yoga: Asanas, Pranayama, Mudras, Mantras

If you can sit quietly, closing your eyes, and breathing deeply, you will probably be able to feel your pulse. If you are still, you might be able to feel the energy buzzing around in your body. That is your Kundalini, looking for an outlet. This deeply revered and universally acknowledged energy that pervades your everyday life is waiting for you to unlock it and let it flow. Your Kundalini is an energy that rests at the bottom of your spine like a small, coiled serpent. When you release this energy, it will flow freely upward through your chakras to give you an expanding state of your consciousness and a deeper connection with the Divine. This is what is known as a Kundalini awakening.

When you awaken your Kundalini, you will be more balanced spiritually and emotionally as well as being more inspired and creative. The energy of the Kundalini supports your spirit and drives all of the everyday functions of your mind and your body. This awakening has been practiced in India for thousands of years and was brought to the western world as a form of yoga practice. The practice of yoga was originally taught to people as a way to find true spiritual enlightenment. Modern yoga is more concerned with poses, but true Kundalini yoga will help you in your quest for true spiritual enlightenment. Kundalini yoga wants to incorporate the focus on all parts of the person into one holistic practice. This means that energy release is taught for the spirit, mind, and body all at the same time. The physical poses will focus on the key points of energy in the body that will activate the areas that need assistance to allow the energy to flow freely. Specific techniques for breathing will help you to unlock your inner energy and learn to control your breathing. The physical part of the Kundalini yoga practice will help you to achieve a heightened sense of awareness. Since your body is a complex system that holds vast systems of energy, it will need specific methods of yoga for energizing it. Kundalini yoga was developed centuries ago for the specific purpose of awakening the Kundalini by opening the internal chakras.

Unlock the Root Chakra with the Crow Pose

Stand straight and tall with your feet close together and your arms stretched out in front of you, palms facing down. Slowly drop to a deep squat, with your bottom almost resting on the floor. Hold it for five seconds and then slowly come back to a standing position. Keep holding your arms straight out in front of you the entire time.

Unlock your Sacral Chakra with the Frog Pose

Leave your toes planted tightly on the ground and lift your heels, keeping them close together. Set your hands on the ground in front of you and look forward. Inhale deeply through your nose and then straighten your knees while you drop your head toward the ground. Then let out your exhale as you drop back into the squat.

Unlock your Solar Plexus Chakra with the Stretch Pose

Lie on your back on the ground or on a yoga mat. Lift your feet about six or seven inches off of the ground and lift your head off the ground. Bring your arms up beside your body so that they are in the air just above the level of your hips. Breathe deeply and slowly.

Unlock your Heart Chakra with the Camel Pose

This pose needs to be done carefully so that you do not strain your lower back. Kneel down on the floor, with your leg from your knee to your feet on the floor. The top part of your feet will be resting flat on the floor. Bend backward slowly and grab your ankles with your hands, allowing your head to drop back and down as far as possible. If you are not able to stretch that far back, then place the palms of your hands on your hips near the small of your back and stretch back only as far as you feel comfortable doing. Keep in mind that there is no best pose, and no one chakra will stand on its own without the others. The entire chakra system works together in an interrelated and holistic system. You can't work on just one of the chakras and ignore the needs of the others. Your Lower Triangle of chakras, the lower three, deal with things that need to be eliminated from your body. The Upper Triangle of the upper three chakras focuses on the accumulation of energy in the body. The two triangles meet in the middle of the body at the Heart Chakra, which works to balance the forces between the chakras.

Asanas

Asana is what we typically think of when we think of yoga. As such, there are hundreds of them, and the proper way to practice them is widely documented and easy to learn. While the details of asana are unnecessary to document here, it is important to understand their specific relationship to the Kundalini awakening. Pranayama is only helpful when it's practiced in the position of an asana. Asana helps to focus the mind by controlling the body and promotes the physical health and circulation necessary for the prana to move freely and the Kundalini to awaken. This bodily focus helps control physical attachments and discomfort that create worldly troubles and make Kundalini's awakening impossible. However, for Kundalini awakening, certain poses are more helpful than others. Simple poses like the lotus position and similar sitting poses are beneficial, and the topsy-turvy and all-members pose, which involve balancing on the head and shoulders, respectively. Asana is one of the best places to start in the journey toward the Kundalini awakening. They lay the groundwork that prepares the body and mind. However, to get the proper benefit from them, they shouldn't be performed as a simple exercise. Practice regularly every day and strive to keep the mind clear and focused on the body's actions.

You'll be able to hold the poses for longer and longer, not merely because your body is becoming more flexible, but also because the mind gains the habit of becoming quiet, still, and patient—free from the passing thoughts and material wants that prevent spiritual awakening.

Pranayama

Pranayama Yoga has a collection of breath-control techniques that are designed to control the vital energy in one's body. One way of making the Kundalini rise is to control the breath. Lie on your back and align your head to the North (some believe that this can facilitate the flow of the Kundalini upwards). Inhale deeply and imagine the Kundalini at the base of your spine glowing brightly. Hold your breath for as long as you can—this is when the energy can slide up. Exhale afterward, then hold it again for as long as possible to make it move some more. After some time, you may be able to feel where the Kundalini is by a warm spot along your spine. Persevere with this method until it reaches the top of your head. Remember to accompany your breaths with visualizations to direct the energy more effectively. The breath is a kind of mechanical push, while the visualization forms the energy according to your instructions.

Mudras

The word mudra has many different meanings, such as "seal" or "closing." While there are many academic as well as intellectual interpretations, the Oral Tradition interprets this as sealing or closing the energy circuits to prevent the energy from being dissipated. Thus, mudras are subtle energy circuits; they are much subtler than the bandhas. You are already aware that you have positive and negative energy from the right and left sides, that is, Pingala and Ida respectively. When the energy circuits are open, the energy does not flow. To understand how these subtle energy circuits function, you must know that the energy flow is categorized according to its qualities. The different fingers of the hand are connected to these qualities.

Anjali Mudra

A well-known mudra that everyone knows and uses for prayer is Anjali Mudra. Anjali means "reverence" or "benediction." In this mudra you hold the palms of your hands together; the two thumbs come together, the forefingers touch each other, the middle finger touches the other middle finger, the ring fingers touch each other as do both the little fingers. When all ten fingers are joined together, all the fine energy circuits are closed and subtle energy can flow.

Jnana Mudra

You are already familiar with Jnana Mudra. After Anjali Mudra this is the most commonly practiced mudra. It is also known as Chit Mudra. Chit means "consciousness." Thus, Chit Mudra is the seal of consciousness. In this mudra, agni (fire) and vayu (air) come together. Since a fire blazes only in the presence of air, one can well imagine that this mudra ignites and sustains a great deal of subtle energy.

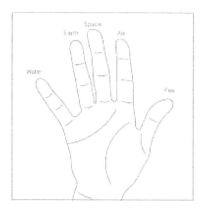

Mantras

According to traditional tantric scriptures, Kundalini energy can be awakened by the recitation of mantras. In this theory, mantras hold a special life force that increases the likelihood of Kundalini awakening with each recitation. In the traditional perspective, this mantra cannot be learned from a book but has to be transmitted by a guru. This is why the practice of mantra recitation is so common in the system of Kundalini yoga created by Yogi Bhajan. It's essentially the full basis for the practice of Transcendental meditation. I personally think that if you find the ritualistic theory of the Kundalini probable and you're interested to awaken your Kundalini by mantra repetition, you should not waste your time repeating a mantra from a book. Instead, get an initiation from a competent teacher. Because according to the tantric model when a teacher gives you a mantra, he essentially infuses his energy onto it. So, you're really not getting the full effect of this practice if you're just repeating a mantra you've learned in a book.

From a more scientific perspective repetition of mantras works as a form of self-hypnosis with positive suggestions. This form of self-hypnosis is relatively safe and will calm most individuals and through that prepare their minds to be more resilient in the face of altered states.

Listening to Mantras

On the other hand, a very passive method of Kundalini awakening, which also was written about in ancient scriptures, is simply listening to mantras. This is actually something every westerner can do by pretty much-buying CDs or mp3s with mantras in them. I personally listen to them all the time because I simply like how they sound.

Chapter 16
Kundalini Energy

Kundalini is a Sanskrit word that can be defined as "coiled up." The origin of this concept is hard to pinpoint, however, it has been found in the ancient Vedic texts of Hindu religions to describe the dormant life-force energy that is present in all humans, and that lies in wait until your "energy" is ready, or has been sparked, to awaken and begin the journey of ascension. Ascension simply means that as you go through the journey of opening your chakras, balancing your energies, and opening your mind and consciousness to higher knowing, you go through a shift or transformation in your dynamic being. Another word to describe ascension might be "evolution," considering it as the evolution of one person's spirit, or soul energy, to transcend and become enlightened. Kundalini energy, that quiet, sleeping spark, is what can often begin the spontaneous clearing and refreshing of all of your chakras. For many people, it can take years of practice and hard work to come into full alignment. The reasons for this are that we are always facing life's challenges, while we are attempting to heal, and it can be difficult to retrain your whole energetic being, consciousness, and physical life, to accommodate a quick and perfunctory evolution. Many people who are eager to heal and transform will work closely with a guru, or teacher, who helps them process the experience of their journey, allowing for more opportunities to push the boundaries and break down the walls and blocks. A teacher is not required or necessary, and you can find your own way of working with this life-force path of ascension, however, you may find that looking for outlets to express your experience to others, or have community during your growth process, as with a teacher or yoga community, will give you a healthier attitude about what you are going through. To understand the basics of Kundalini, imagine a snake coiled up in your pelvic bowl. It was there when you were conceived and growing inside of your mother's womb and it has its presence in your life energy, without even realizing it is there. The "snake" of energy is the life spark, that when pushed out of its slumber will entice and invigorate an abrupt shift in the energy of your life.

Bringing yourself into a higher consciousness comes from this coiled energy, uncoiling and rising up through your chakras, reaching the crown of your head and opening up your whole being. Some gurus or Kundalini practitioners posit that the energy then must cycle back down to the root chakra at the end of the spinal cord, where it begins its journey and where it lies dormant so that you can fully face the whole cycle of coming into your purest energetic being. As you expose yourself to these concepts, you may wonder why this energy is dormant to start with, and why it would awaken at all.

Why Does It "Awaken"?

When you are born, you do not know who you are and where you just were before. You are innocent, pure, and helpless and you learn everything one moment at a time in your life through the environment you are in, through your inherent nature and personality, and through the way you care for right from the start. For some people, this can mean that you will have a lot of ease, support, caring fathers and mothers, and a good deal of healthy and secure attachment so that you can successfully incorporate your personality, beliefs, and passions into the world. For others, it can be a harder road that involves a lot of falling down, hard times, lack of early life nurturing, dealing with trauma and pain, and learning that it isn't secure for you to be who you truly are, deep down inside. The reasons that people go through an evolution or ascension experience are entirely unique to the individual and it doesn't hinge on whether you had a good upbringing or a challenging one. All people have the potential to experience a Kundalini Awakening journey. In some cases, you will find that through your own spiritual journey, or quest for enlightenment, you come across yoga practices, meditations, and other forms of "opening" that will connect you to a higher power within yourself, or that will promote your choice to discover more than what is obvious or seen in our world. This is the reason that people devote their lives to practicing certain religions and philosophies. Take a Buddhist monk as an example: their entire life's devotion is understanding life through the experience of worship of certain energies, deities, and the experience of ascending to a place of total enlightenment. We are not all intended for that life and yet we all have the power to become personally enlightened to understand a deeper sense of truth from within, and about the universe as a whole. The Kundalini energy wants to wake up when you are ready and/or willing to ascend and bring your full life force into this world. In a lot of ways, people prevent this ignition from occurring. It can be very frightening to change your beliefs or ideas about the world or about who you perceive you are as an individual. It can be a long and intense journey that is easy to avoid with distractions, substances, denial, and a vast array of other means of escape. So, where does all of that fear come from, that fear of awakening? A lot of the time it can come from blocks in several of your chakras. Your energy may have a desire to open up, but if you can't or won't, then you will continue to keep your "snake" coiled at the root of your energy system. In a lot of instances of awakening, it has been known to appear out of nowhere for a person and can be very uncomfortable or feel like you are having a "nervous breakdown." We are not all educated to know about the chakras and Kundalini and so when it manifests in our energetic reality without knowledge of what it is, the reaction can be to suppress it, avoid it, call it names like "insanity" or "illness," when in reality, it is your body, mind, and spirit starting to align and become an evolved and enlightened entity. The reason your Kundalini energy wants to awaken is so that you can ascend as a being of Earth and become in full attunement with your purest nature as a person of energetic light. You can ask it to open through a lot of practice and focused intention, or you can be surprised by its opening up, seemingly out of nowhere. When it does come up without intention or focus, it can happen as the result of a traumatic experience, like loss, grief, or mental/emotional/physical abuse, as well as self-inflicted abuse, such as with drugs and alcohol. For many people, the experience is challenging, no matter how it arrives and presents itself. The power of this energy is how you get to understand your true nature, your wisdom, your inner light, and your purpose for being alive. It is either a choice you make, to awaken the snake, or the choice is made anyway, whether you mentally ask for it, or not. It is your inner power that wants to rise and ascend through you, aligning your whole energetic system to your mind and your body so that you can become a wholly enlightened being. Many people will never experience Kundalini awakening in their lifetimes and it is due to a lack of interest or awareness in such causes. If you are reading this book, then you are looking for a higher knowing and are likely ready to start this empowering journey to your truest self. Your body comes equipped with seven physical energy centers that you will likely experience in your Kundalini awakening. While there are many chakras associated with each soul, these seven chakras are the ones associated with the physical body. Each chakra has a different color, location, and design. They are as follows: The first chakra is the root chakra which is located by the tailbone. This chakra is red and is responsible for our connection to Earth. We ground through our root chakra by connecting our energy to Earth energy. It keeps our multi-dimensional soul-self firmly planted on our home planet.

The second chakra is the sacral chakra which is located below your belly button. This chakra is orange and is associated with all of our sexual organs. It is responsible for creation. All of our personal creations manifest in the sacral chakra. The third chakra is the solar plexus chakra. This chakra is yellow exists in your solar plexus, located below your rib cage. The solar plexus chakra is often called our seat of power, as this is the center of our physical being. Here, we come to know ourselves and our true nature. We develop confidence, authenticity, and a clear knowing of self through this chakra.

The fourth chakra is the heart chakra. This chakra is located over your heart and is represented by the color green. It is responsible for our ability to love and empathically connect to ourselves and those around us. We experience emotion through the heart chakra. It allows us to remember that we are all one. The fifth chakra is the throat chakra. This blue chakra is located in the throat but also accounts for the mouth as it is linked with our capacity to speak nothing but veracity. The throat chakra allows us to remember what we are here to do and communicate that with others. It helps us speak honestly and purely to those around us, with kindness, thoughtfulness, and love. It also helps us stand up for ourselves and others.

The sixth chakra is the third eye chakra. This indigo chakra is located directly between and slightly above your eyebrows. It is responsible for helping you see and interact with the spiritual world through your physical senses. The senses we experience and interpret concerning the third eye are often called the Clair senses. They represent a metaphysical extension of our physical senses, allowing us to experience more than the physical consciousness can experience on its own.

The seventh chakra is your crown chakra. This chakra is positioned above the top of your head and is represented by the color violet. Opposite the root chakra, this chakra is responsible for your ability to connect to the source. It allows you to stay attuned to source energy in your physical body.

Now that you understand the seven basic physical chakras, let's take a look at how these chakras are affected by Kundalini energy.

Chapter 17
Reiki Healing

How Reiki Healing Works: The Theory

When looked at from the most obvious level, it is clear that Reiki treatment has a direct impact on lowering stress levels and releasing tension from the system. Further than this, it also helps a person move towards a better balance in body, mind, and spirit. Even more, it can help the body's own natural healing mechanisms kick in again and begin to function more effectively.

What Exactly Is Reiki Doing?

So, the question is, how does Reiki lower stress and help enable the body to heal? An exact answer to this question remains to be found. However, there have been increasing levels of research covering the effects of Reiki. There is now evidence showing its effect on lowering heart rate, blood pressure, and stress hormones. It has also been exhibited to improve immune strength. While we have evidence to show the effects Reiki has, we can only offer broad theories as to what causes these effects and how exactly the healing is occurring. Reiki affects us on multiple levels and often with immediate results. This suggests that Reiki is a complex process that interacts with many of the body's systems simultaneously. It results in the body shifting from a stressed state, also known as fight-or-flight mode, to one of relaxation, where the body is primed to heal itself—this is referred to as a parasympathetic state. Many scientists suggest that this shift is triggered on a subconscious level in an area referred to as the biofield.

What Is the Biofield?

The biofield refers to an area that surrounds the physical body. Medical science has adopted the term to explain the vibrational energy field that is believed to exist in this space. There is no way of actually studying the biofield as current technology is not yet capable of verifying its existence. Having said this, traditional and indigenous cultures have recognized this biofield of energy for thousands of years, and it has always been believed to be a cornerstone of health and wellbeing. Any disruption to this biofield was seen as a loss in balance and the beginning of an illness. So, just because science has not developed far enough to examine this phenomenon, it does not mean it should be dismissed. The wisdom from indigenous cultures runs much deeper than science, which is a relatively new faculty in terms of human history. Many healing traditions from indigenous cultures use vibration to restore the necessary balance to the mind and body. We can see evidence of this in practices such as ceremonial drumming, chanting rituals, and humming. There is a lot of science to support the therapeutic benefits of vibration through music and sounds. This has led musicians to purposely construct music that can raise or lower people's energies to the desired level. One song called Weightless was developed by Marconi Union to help relieve stress.

The song is said to decrease stress levels by up to 60% once listened to with closed eyes. You can feel the vibrational shift through listening to the song as your body's natural rhythm realigns itself. Some say that Reiki's healing benefits are derived from a similar vibrational mechanism, one which increases the level of coherence in the body and decreases the level of dissonance. Another theory suggests that a Reiki practitioner's hands hold the power of the energetic vibrations which are transmitted to the recipient. These vibrations are then passed from the practitioner to the client to induce healing. The effect could then cause the client to have a shift in awareness as they recognize the healing power, they hold within is the key to their wellbeing, regardless of their current state of health. Reiki could then be seen as helping a person resync back to health, similar to how grandfather clocks in the same room adjust to the rhythm of the main clock or how we, too, become relaxed in the presence of someone who is very peaceful. Reiki can connect the practitioner with a deep, inner peace regardless of how they are feeling at that moment. Many other therapies aim to restore the biofield balance. These include yoga, acupuncture, qigong, and shiatsu to name but a few. Reiki is one of the most subtle of these therapies as it uses mainly vibrations rather than physical manipulation or even gentle force. It is also suggested by some that Reiki does not act in the biofield at all but rather another field known as the unified field. Some believe that Reiki is more similar to meditation than other energy therapies.

Reiki Compared to Other Treatments

According to the NCCIH, Reiki is an alternative medicine practice that complements existing practices by using energy that is still to be measured by science. Most energy healing methods presume that humans inhabit a certain type of energy that both runs through us and around us. It is believed that energy therapies such as Healing Touch help to bring equilibrium to these energies. As mentioned, many Reiki practitioners see Reiki as completely distinct to most energy healing and more akin to meditative practices. Many energy healing methods use specific ways to gain access to a person's biofield to make alterations; Reiki does not try to diagnose problems or purposely alter the energy field. They are more passive in their involvement as the energy finds its path. Reiki practice by nature is extremely passive. A practitioner's hand does not move for most of the treatment duration. The only time they do is alter placements of the hands. A Reiki practitioner is a neutral party; they do not try to change a person or change their energy field. A Reiki practitioner does not try to harness and use Reiki energy; they simply rest their hands on a person's body. Sometimes, they will rest their hands just above the body, in cases where there is an open wound or burn that needs to be healed.

The energy that arises in a practitioner's hands comes naturally as it responds to the needs of the individual for balance in certain areas. Because of this, every treatment is tailored to meet the specific needs of that person, although the practitioner often uses a similar process for every session. Reiki is best administered in a complete session; however, it can also be given in a shorter session to tackle certain points of a person's body. In pressing circumstances, even a few minutes of Reiki makes a big difference.

How Reiki Healing Is Done: The Healing Session

Reiki session has no standard or even a set time limit or exact protocol to be adhered to. It is allowed to be performed by anyone who has received the necessary training. This might be someone who is professionally qualified, but it can also be a healthcare provider or a friend or member of your family; it could even be you.

There is also no typical setting required for Reiki. Generally, Reiki works best somewhere quiet, but it can be performed anywhere, regardless of what is going on in the vicinity and no matter what is happening to the person receiving it. A few moments of Reiki often bring relaxation to emergencies. It is often administered directly after injuries occur and even during and after surgeries.

Who Should I See?

To give yourself the best experience possible, you must take the time to do some research before choosing a practitioner that you believe you can be comfortable with. You should decide whether you want to receive Reiki from a friend or a professional you do not know. If you have a friend that you feel very comfortable with, it can help improve the bonding experience. However, if you are not naturally comfortable with strangers, you may want to choose a professional for a greater level of experience. Try to meet with your practitioner beforehand to get a feel for the person and to know what to expect from the session. Look for a practitioner who describes the process to you clearly and details how they plan to structure the session. This will help you know what to expect when going into the session, and it will make you more at ease. Your personal experience of Reiki will be very different from most others, but if you know what to expect before going in, it always helps.

What Is the Setting?

The most beneficial setting is one where it is quiet and where you will not be disturbed. Most professional Reiki practitioners will have a space dedicated to their practice. If they are doing house calls, they will usually have plenty of knowledge of how best to set up an optimal space. Practitioners often play soft music during sessions to promote relaxation through ambient sounds. If you prefer to have no music, however, do not be afraid to let your practitioner know.

The length of sessions can vary widely. For those receiving Reiki in hospitals and nursing homes, sessions tend to only last around twenty minutes. Professional practitioners provide treatments that last up to ninety minutes. Most Reiki treatments are in between the two.

What Is Involved in a Session?

A full Reiki session requires the recipient to be lying down or upright in a comfortable chair. Usually, Reiki is performed with soft touches, where the practitioner's hands are placed in multiple locations. These include the head and front and back of a person's belly area. A practitioner should not put their hands in private places, and they should not feel intrusive. Extra placements on injured parts of the body may be performed as needed, such as on the arm for a surgical scar. The practitioner can also hold their hands just above the affected area if it is sore to the touch, providing the same treatment benefits.

What Is the Experience Like?

The experience of Reiki is very subjective. Sometimes, the changes are very subtle and not initially noticeable to the recipient. However, there seems to be an array of shared experiences many people feel during a Reiki treatment. Some people quote a feeling of heat emanating from the practitioner's hands, while others note a refreshingly cool feeling coming from their hands. Some also experience a pulsating effect where the practitioner's hands are placed as waves of energy pulsate and flow through the body. A lot of people comment on how comforting the experience is. One study reported how recipients regularly felt that they were hovering in an altered state of consciousness while, at the same time, being fully aware of their surroundings and drawn deeply within. Others have reported falling into a deep, meditative state, while some find the experience to be quite dramatic. Some find their first Reiki session to be not very eventful, but they often report feeling good afterward. The usual resulting feeling is one of deep relaxation and an instant release of stress.

Reiki is a compounding practice and even those who do not notice much on their first time, usually get deeper and more profound experiences as they continue their sessions. Aside from the immediate after-effects of Reiki treatment, you may also experience other positive changes in the days afterward. These include better digestion, a more centered feeling as opposed to being reactive, and better and deeper sleep.

Chapter 18
Spiritual Awakening vs. Kundalini Awakening: What's the Difference

Spiritual awakening is not the same as Kundalini awakening. While both forms of awakening are attempts to move one's energy inwards, spiritual awakening is purely mental whereas Kundalini Awakening involves physical and mental energy.

According to the Kundalini Research and Enlightenment Foundation, kundalini as a practice has an orientation towards spiritual enlightenment and liberation, while kundalini yoga as a practice may be oriented towards physical and mental liberation.

In Hindu philosophy, Kundalini Awakening (or Kundalini Yoga) is the process of awakening of kundalini energy in a human being from within through pranayama, meditation, and asceticism. It is said to lead to the spiritual awakening of all beings and liberation.

Spiritual awakening comes about through connection to our own inner divinity and higher knowledge discovered through intuition, mindfulness, and self-reflection.

Spiritual awakening describes the realization that you are not your physical form or ego, and the subsequent freedom from suffering and joy that comes with this realization. Unlike Kundalini Awakening, spiritual awakening is purely mental, which means it can be achieved by anyone regardless of his or her religious beliefs or background. In fact, many people experience spiritual awakening long before they ever try an energy-raising practice.

To achieve spiritual awakening, you must understand that your ego exists in the first place. Your ego is that part of yourself that you believe to be your personality and self-identity at any given moment. For example, when you are sad, your ego believes it is sad. When you are happy, your ego believes it is happy.

When you achieve spiritual awakening, you realize that your ego doesn't actually exist at all. In fact, everything that makes up your current illusion of reality stems from the identity and thoughts that make up your ego. When you break free from identifying with your ego's thoughts and identity, then no longer will you be able to suffer from unhappiness or dissatisfaction.

A kundalini awakening is the awakening of the kundalini energy at the base of the spine. It initiates a process in which the kundalini rises up the spine through the various chakras to the top of the head. This process normally takes many lifetimes to complete. The kundalini process is associated with the process of enlightenment, which brings greater light into the subtle energy body and ends in enlightenment.

The journey of kundalini continues from wherever the kundalini left off in the former lifetime. So, if in the last lifetime the kundalini had risen to the heart chakra, then it will be rising from there in the next lifetime. Generally speaking, a soul's spiritual development is marked by the level to which kundalini has risen.

The kundalini process varies greatly in every individual. Kundalini may get stuck in a chakra for many lifetimes, or it may rise through one or more chakras in one lifetime. It can even fall back down into lower chakras. Its progress depends on many factors, some of which are under one's control and some not.

This is a complex subject, which I'm not going to address any further here except to say that the spiritual path is often rocky and difficult and also guided beautifully and perfectly as a result of kundalini's movement. The kundalini process is the spiritual process, and it proceeds as it will and as it needs to in a somewhat predictable, yet individual, way. This process is guided by the soul and by the nonphysical beings who carry out the soul's plan. This process is not up to one's individual will. In fact, willfulness often causes trouble in this process, which requires surrender, not will.

There's no rushing this process, although many things such as meditation support it and ensure a smoother process. Pushing kundalini farther than it's meant to go is unwise. Some spiritual practices attempt to do this but at a cost. This can lead to an unbalanced individual: someone who has advanced spiritually or who has psychic powers without sufficient integrity and embodiment of the Truth. This is something occult practitioners often dabble in, and it is ill-advised. Everything has its own timing, and kundalini will awaken naturally and probably smoothly when your soul is ready to step onto the spiritual path.

The Main Differences Between Spiritual Awakening and Kundalini Awakening

Spiritual Awakening Is Mental, Kundalini Awakening Is Physical and Mental

Spiritual awakening means that you have an awareness or remembrance of oneness and divine intelligence that is always present and within your own mind and body. It is about recognizing that you are the same as the universe, or God, or whatever term one wishes to use to describe this Oneness. Kundalini awakening on the other hand is a physical and mental process that involves a movement of energy from within your body or up your spine to awaken kundalini shakti.

Kundalini Awakening Is Aligned with Religion, Spiritual Awakening Isn't

Spiritual awakening is an extremely personal and internal experience while kundalini awakening is a physical process. To some degree, the kundalini awakening process is also spiritual, given that this type of awakening is an attempt to awaken the spirit within oneself. However, it does not require one to have a religious or spiritual background to achieve this type of awareness.

In fact, many people have been able to achieve spiritual awakening before they ever even think about kundalini awakening, and some of them never even try an energy-raising practice.

Kundalini Awakening Is Aligned with Some Spiritual Practices, Spiritual Awakening Isn't

Spiritual awakening is a purely mental experience whereas kundalini awakening involves physical and mental energy. This distinction can be seen in the structure of these two types of awakening.

The kundalini awakening process requires one to perform physical and mental practices such as yoga, meditation, and breath retention. By comparison, spiritual awakening is a purely mental experience.

Kundalini Awakening Is Aligned with Some Religious Beliefs, Spiritual Awakening Isn't

Compared to spiritual awakening, kundalini awakening is extremely personal and it also involves a belief system. Spiritually awakening means that you understand that Oneness and divine intelligence is always present and within your own mind and body. However, when it comes to kundalini awakening, it requires a belief system to work.

Spiritual awakening may sometimes be confused with kundalini awakening because both types of awakening involve the experience of Oneness and divine intelligence. However, there are many differences between the two practices.

Chapter 19
Spiritual Awakening vs. Enlightenment

While the terms "spiritual awakening" and "enlightenment" are used interchangeably in popular culture, they do have distinct meanings. In essence, an awakening (or spiritual awakening) is a period of spiritual and religious revelation during which one is suddenly aware of what formerly seemed to be just intuition or insight. However, enlightenment can be achieved in any given lifetime and isn't necessarily connected with a spiritual event; it refers to a state of understanding independent from religion or faith.

"Enlightenment" is the result of a spiritual awakening. The Enlightenment was an intellectual movement in Western Europe and North America in the 18th century, originating from French, German, and Scottish thinkers of the Age of Enlightenment. It began in France during the 1780s after the end of the French Revolution and gained momentum in the 20th century with Isaac Bashevis Singer's 1968 novel "The Letter Writer."

In an intellectual sense, enlightenment is defined as the development of the fullest human capacity for self-aware (or independent) thought. With this understanding, enlightened individuals have a better understanding of the world and know more about it than those without such knowledge. They then use their knowledge to overcome ignorance and achieve what is often called "spiritual experiences" or "peak experiences." Though, it can be said that nobody is completely enlightened; rather, people are only at a certain level in their life journey and growth.

Religious principles and practices are the core of spiritual awakening, which can be defined as a bringing forth of heightened spiritual thought into one's everyday life. A spiritual awakening can provoke a person to begin practicing religious rituals as a way of life. It is also characterized by an increased awareness of spirituality and the transcendental world (i.e., the feeling that we live more than one life or that there is something permanent in our lives). Spiritual awakenings can also lead people to try to escape the earthly world, causing them to neglect their physical health.

Enlightenment is described as a sudden awakening to what is ultimately real, though some believe that it can be achieved through a gradual process of realization. Enlightenment can be defined as a more advanced state of spiritual awakening, in which one begins to understand the interconnectedness of all things. In contrast to spiritual awakenings, enlightenment is not affected by one's personal experience.

To be spiritually awakened is to experience the divine through one's heightened awareness. One who is awakened will have a deeper understanding and connection with their soul (or spirit), perhaps even experiencing a feeling of love and devotion toward some form of God or higher power. The person will be more aware of the fact that they are a spirit and not just a human. In being awakened, they see the world in a new light and have an increased respect for life.

Enlightenment is the ultimate state of human consciousness. It is a perfect state of omniscience, omnipresence, and omnipotence. Enlightenment cannot be achieved as it already occupies the entire space of one's existence. However, enlightenment can be experienced here and now through various practices and methods. Buddhist practitioners call this state 'Dharma-kaya. Enlightenment is experienced through prana (energy) which connects one with the universal consciousness. In its most basic form, enlightenment can be explored through four 'paramitas' or 'perfections.' These are the four seals of Buddhism that make up the foundation of its belief system. They are the perfection of giving, the perfection of morality, the perfection of patience, and the perfection of meditation.

Amida Buddha has been enlightened through the four paramitas. To help others, attain enlightenment Amida Buddha appeared in this world. This accounts for why Amida is worshiped as a savior and a god in Buddhism as well as why he is referred to as Tathagata (a title for Buddha). "Tathagata" literally translates as "one who has arrived at enlightenment." There are four major Buddhist traditions, or "sangha," within Buddhism. The first tradition is the Theravada, which is more commonly referred to as the Thai Forest Tradition. The second tradition is the Mahayana, which is more commonly referred to as the Pure Land Tradition. The third tradition is known as Vajrayana or Tantrayana and it can be found in many different forms in Tibetan Buddhism, Shinto Buddhism, and Esoteric Buddhism. The fourth is known as Khon dharma.

The four major traditions differ on the issue of Pure Land Buddhism. Some will strongly disagree with some other schools' view of the Pure Land, while others may tend to agree with the other schools' point of view. Theravada does not believe in Amitabha Buddha's past lives and that he has no prior life deeds to be born over and over again as a human, animal, or ghost. It is Theravada's view that Amida Buddha is a savior and that he has saved all of mankind from the sufferings of samsara (cyclic existence), which is the Buddhist term for reincarnation, during his lives in the Tusita Heaven. However, Theravada also believes that one can attain Nirvana without mediation. This belief views the Buddha as an ordinary human being, and not a god. Theravada Buddhism is known for its strict adherence to monasticism and emphasizes the practice of meditation. Mahayana Buddhism tends to believe that Amida Buddha has lived numerous lives as both a god and a human, though it still believes in Amitabha Buddha's many past lives to judge his enlightenment after he died. It also believes that Amida is not above humans and behaves like them. Mahayana also uses the term 'tathagata' to refer to Buddha, but it uses this term in the sense that Amida is a being who has become enlightened and will not fall back into a state of samsara. Mahayana also believes that one can attain Nirvana without mediation, however, it is said that by following the teachings of Buddha one will surely attain Buddhahood. Mahayana Buddhism is more focused on Amida Buddha and more willing to worship him as a god. Vajrayana Buddhism focuses on the teachings and practices of the Karma Kagyu School. The third tradition speaks for itself in terms of the title. Vajrayana means 'Diamond Vehicle' and represents a pure form of Buddhism, for only those who have a very strong will can attain enlightenment. It is based on the notion of 'three bodies' (trikaya), which represents the past lives and loves being taken by Buddha. Vajrayana also focuses on the concept of propitiation, for it believes that a Bodhisattva of Amida Buddha can be seen as a manifestation of the Buddha himself when he is in his khoryinya (the highest) body. However, because Vajrayana Buddhism is so heavily rooted in faith and in its various forms it is considered to be more concerned with ritualism than meditation.

The four major Buddhist traditions differ on what they consider to be the 'enlightened' state. The Theravada believes that ordinary human beings will not reach Nirvana until they can be reborn into the Tusita Heaven. However, it is believed that during rebirth one's karma can be transformed into virtue resulting in a 'better rebirth', or even after death one can be reborn into the Tusita Heaven. While the Mahayana believes that all of mankind will eventually attain enlightenment in Amitabha Buddha's Pure Land and all of those who attain Buddhahood in his Pure Land are bodhisattvas.

Mahayana believes that all of mankind can attain enlightenment in the Pure Land, but it also believes that one can attain Nirvana without mediation. This belief is based on the notion that if a person practices enough they will eventually reach a state of samadhi (a state of mind). However, Mahayana also believes that if Amida or any bodhisattva were to return from Pure Land before one's death then the person who died first would be reborn into the Pure Land as a bodhisattva. However, Mahayana also believes that one can avoid certain deaths and therefore avert the descent of Amida into a realm. This is achieved by performing as many good deeds as possible and sins and negative thoughts are removed by faith in Amida

Buddha. Vajrayana Buddhism also believes in 'enlightenment without mediation.' However, this belief is based on the concept that since all beings are already enlightened or have like potential (such as being a bodhisattva), they must go through the process of attaining enlightenment. In fact, if one were to be reborn as a human and attain enlightenment without mediation then they would return to the land of Amida Buddha and be reborn again as a bodhisattva. Vajrayana also believes that if a bodhisattva is reborn in Pure Land by returning from an immeasurable light, then they must return to this world again for 'other beings.' However, Vajrayana also believes that this world can be saved and that all human beings should strive towards enlightenment.

Buddhist teachings emphasize the importance of enlightenment and rebirth. Buddhists are taught that mankind is inherently good and inspired by a common ideal. Buddhists believe that everyone has within them a Buddha-nature (innate or natural potential to attain enlightenment). The Buddha-nature, or enlightenment, is not something that is awakened over decades of meditation but is rather something worth striving for. In Mahayana Buddhism, this nature becomes a focus of practice called bodhicitta. The purpose of Mahayana is to lead all human beings towards the attainment of Bodhi (enlightenment).

Buddhism differs from other religions in that it does not explain the nature of spiritual awakening. It believes that all people are already inherently enlightened by the attainment of buddha nature and it is therefore not necessary for everyone to have a distinct experience of enlightenment.

Chapter 20
Breathing Techniques

Breath is significantly important to the quality of your energy and your chakras. Breath is life and the force that engages the flow of energy through your chakra system. The final narrative offers you a series of breathing exercises for each chakra, designed to help you keep balance as you practice living with your energy. Each of these exercises may be added to your lessons and meditations. I strongly encourage you to commit to using these breathing techniques regularly. You can do them in the morning before work, or at the end of the day to clear all of the energy from your daily life or work schedule. They can be used in place of your yoga or fitness routine and can be a good way for you to practice your energy clearing techniques regularly. Bring breath to your chakras and awaken your energy within!

Breath for the Root Chakra

1. Sitting on the floor, stretch your legs straight in front of you. Be sure to keep your back straight.

2. Place your hands to your shoulders and push your elbows out to the side in line with your shoulders.

3. Breath slowly in through your nose. Lift your arms overhead and pull your knees up to your chest so they are pointing upward toward the sky. Make certain that your feet stay flat on the floor and keep your sacrum planted to the ground while you reach up.

4. Begin to release your breath and lower your legs down, back into a straight position. Keep your spine straight while you bring your hands back to their original position on your shoulders, elbows pointed to the sides.

5. Repeat this cycle several times. If you feel comfortable, you can gain momentum, but be sure to keep in your comfort zone.

6. Remember to practice seeing yourself rooted to the earth as you practice this exercise.

7. Ending this exercise, pull your legs into a cross-legged position. Feel the energy of your root chakra and consider it for as long as you need.

Breath for the Sacral Chakra

1. Sit on the floor and draw your knees into your chest. Place your hands on the front of your knees. Your knees do not have to be against your chest, just slightly out from you, feet flat on the floor.

2. Breathe in through your nose and pull your sacrum forward, tilting your pelvis to make a curve in your lower back. Use your hands against the front of your knees to support your back.

3. Open your chest upward to the sky as you are pulling yourself forward and arching your back.

4. Breathe out and reverse the action to push the curve back, drawing your navel toward your spine and reversing the curve of your spine.

5. Bring your legs into a cross-legged position and shut your eyes. Return to a normal breathing cycle. Meditate on the energy stirred and awakened in your sacral chakra and relax here for as long as you need.

Breath for the Solar Plexus Chakra

1. Position your body in the same position you did for the second chakra. Place your hands gently on the front of your knees keeping them pulled close to your chest with your back straight.

2. Bent your back and pull your abdomen ahead pushing your navel forward. Keep your back supported by keeping a hold of your knees with your hands.

3. Roll your torso from over to the left side, continuing all the way around. Pull your belly button back into your spine and continue rolling back around to the front with your navel pushed forward. The idea is to create a smooth, circle roll.

4. Repeat this circle roll around starting from the front to the left side, and then back to the right side. Repeat several times.

5. Repeat again going in the opposite direction, several times.

6. You can gradually pick up speed but only if it feels comfortable for your spine. Don't overdo it and keep it slow if you need to limit your spinal movement.

7. The importance of this exercise is that you maintain focus on your breathing. Try to breathe in for the belly forward position, and then breathe out as you reach the navel-back position. Breathe in from the front to left to side, and breathe out from the back to right side, breathe in front...and so on.

Breath for the Heart Chakra

1. Sit with legs crossed on the floor or sit in a chair. Place your hands on your shoulders and push your elbows out so they are pointed to the side.

2. Take a slow and deep breath in. Twist your body to the right and lengthen and straighten your spine as you twist. Keep your abdominal muscles engaged.

3. Breathe out slowly and twist your body all the way over to the left. Remember to keep your back straight and long. Engage your abdominal muscles engaged and chest wide open. Try not to arch your back.

4. Keep the breaths in and out slow and deep.

5. Bring your back to a normal resting position. Drop your hands down to your knees and breathe normally, keeping your eyes closed.

6. Consider the energy of your heart and reflect on the feelings, thoughts, or emotions that come up for as long as you need.

Breath for the Throat Chakra

1. Sit with your legs crossed on the floor, or in a chair keeping your spine long.

2. Interlace your fingers together and clasp your hands together. Keep your elbows pointing down towards your navel and touching together at their points. Place your clasped hands under your chin.

3. Inhale long and deep and push your elbows out to the side. Keep your fingers under the chin and woven together.

4. Letting the breath out, lift your chin and push your elbows back together. Keep your fingers as they were under your chin. Open your mouth and tilt your head back. Stick your tongue out for an extra stretch.

5. Make an audible sound while you breathe out. Any sound will do. Let it come naturally to you.

6. Repeat this cycle of breath and motion several times.

7. Bring your head back to a normal resting position and breathe normally. Rest your hands in your lap, or on your knees. Consider the energy pulled into your throat chakra and listen to the energy of your throat chakra for as long as you need.

Breath for the Brow Chakra

1. Sit on the floor with your legs crossed or upright in a chair with your eyes closed. Focus attention on your breath.

2. While breathing, envision opening a curtain or drapes hanging in front of your third eye to let light in. Imagine the drapes from your living room or bedroom if it helps you find the image you need.

3. Breathe in through your nose and then reach your hands out in front of you. Stretch your fingers wide and then open your eyes as wide as you can.

4. Reach your arms to the side while you hold your breath. Imagine as you reach your arms to the side that you are throwing the curtains open in front of a window. See a light, image, or color as you "open the drapes."

5. Breathing out, bring your hands to your face and cover your eyes. Picture in your brow chakra the image, shape, color, or light that you envisioned with your eyes opened.

6. Repeat this cycle several times.

7. Return your breath to a normal pace for you. Rest your hands on your lap. Keeping your eyes closed, focus on your visualization. Practice seeing with your eyes closed.

Breath for the Crown

1. Sit on a stool or on the floor with legs crossed. Keep your spine long and chest open. Place your hands on your knees. Begin to concentrate on your breathing.

2. Places your palms together with your fingers pointed toward your chin and placed in front of your heart chakra.

3. Draw in a long, deep breath and then reach your arms and fingers up toward the sky with your palms still pressed together.

4. Breathe out and reach your hands out to your sides in line with your shoulders.

5. Place your hands back in the prayer position in front of your heart. Begin your next breath in and start the next cycle over.

6. Repeat this exercise several times.

7. To finish this breathing exercise, place your hands back in your lap, or on your knees and breath normally. Keep your spine straight. Reflect for however long you need to be silent and still.

Chapter 21
Guided Meditation for Beginners

What Meditation Really Is

Just like the very concept of the third eye itself, there are so many misconceptions surrounding the idea of meditation. To many, meditation is sitting cross-legged on the floor for hours on end, either trying to empty your mind of all thoughts or trying to focus on a certain idea, word, or concept (the mantra). This description is only partially correct and describes only a shadow of what meditation is supposed to be.

We've already tackled the third eye—the Ajna chakra—which opens up the full potential of the mind. The true purpose of meditation is to allow this to happen. Consider the idea of building a house. The opened third eye is the house itself, and your mind is the place where it will be built. However, it's very impractical to build a house on an unkempt lot. The ground needs to be cleared, and the foundation has to be laid. This is the purpose of meditation—to make our minds more receptive to the changes and benefits that opening the third eye brings.

Given this, meditation is not just about "clearing." It's more about preparing. When you build a house, you need to take stock of the soil, the quality of the earth, the integrity of the lot, and the availability of surrounding resources. In short, you get to know the land, in essence connecting to it.

This is exactly what meditation is about. Like Pranayama and other breathing exercises, it's just a means, not an end. But while breathing is a means to enrich the body and calm the mind, meditation is a means to strengthen the spirit by connecting to one's sense of self. When one's third eye is opened, the person suddenly becomes aware of the whole self. But sometimes this self is not the entity that one expects to know. No matter how well we think of ourselves, there are always aspects of our personality that we are either unaware of, or unable to accept. Maybe there are flaws or opportunities that we find. When we open our third eye without the benefits that meditation has to offer, we get blindsided and ultimately inundated by the unexpected totality of our personalities. As mentioned before, at this point the downsides of opening the third eye outweigh the good.

Meditation 101: The Passive Mind

One of the easiest forms of meditation—and one that trains us to realize the self as the container of the other aspects we attribute to our personality—is that which teaches the mind to passively observe the thoughts and emotions that come to it is the contemplative equivalent of the exercise we had earlier, where you imagined yourself sitting in a park. You watch the other people all around you, but you do not interact with them. In the same vein, in this meditation, you watch the thoughts that come and go through your mind, but you do not interact with them. The idea of non-interaction is key here. A busy mind grabs at each thread of thought that enters it, weaving it into anything from questions and ideas to worries and concerns. Sometimes this is useful, such as when doing creative thinking or problem-solving. But for our purposes, the mind needs to be quiet. And instead of forcing it to shut the thoughts out as in more advanced meditative practices, we will train it first to keep itself in check. It is far easier to work on our mind, rather than on our thoughts!

Here's how you embark on this passive-mind exercise:

- Sit comfortably. Ideally, sit cross-legged on the floor—this helps ensure you don't fall off a chair while meditating. But if sitting cross-legged is not comfortable, you may also sit on a cushioned chair with a tall back and armrests, so that it can completely support you.
- To measure your progress, you may want to have a stopwatch or timer nearby. Start the time once you are ready to meditate.

- Close your eyes. If you need, you may also use earplugs (especially if you can't find someplace with a noise level conducive to meditation).

- Breathe in and out for about a minute. There's no need to count the seconds, as the purpose of the breaths is to calm your mind. Stop only when you feel sufficiently calm and relaxed.

- After focusing on breathing, focus on the thoughts that come to your mind. Imagine that you are standing in the middle of a field, with thoughts swimming in the air in front of you. Visualize yourself looking at the thoughts, as if looking at fish in an aquarium. As you do, take care not to "catch" or indulge the thoughts. You might, for example, encounter a thought about something you ought to do later in the day. Normally, the mind would take that thought and spin it into a plan on how to accomplish it or worry about what would happen if you failed to complete it. Don't let this develop—instead, let the thought be. Let it enter your awareness, and just watch it swim past you as other thoughts take their place.

- Some thoughts will be stronger than others. The more the thought means to you, the more it will draw you in. Naturally, you find yourself distracted at first, especially while you're still in the early stages.

- If you do find yourself drawn to a thought, dissociate yourself from it. You may resume the visualization of the thoughts swimming around you, or you may visualize yourself slowly moving away from the thought and back into the field where you were before.

- Stay in this passive space in your mind for as long as you can. Remember, you should feel relaxed while doing this. Trying too hard to stay in this space will stress you out. After the initial effort of getting into this space, it should come naturally. If not, slowly ease yourself out of this space and try again after a minute.

- You may find it useful to transition from your regular mental state to a meditative state by slowly counting backward from 10. As you do, envision yourself moving through a tunnel or a corridor, with your desired mental state at the destination (the field of thoughts when starting, and your current location when ending your meditation.

- After your practice, end the timer and log how many minutes you were able to sustain your meditation. Don't be discouraged if you can't do it for long yet—that's natural. But as you do this every day, aim to beat the former day's record.

- The ultimate goal of this exercise is to be able to enter the passive mind state at will. As you go through your practice, you will notice the various benefits of passively viewing your thoughts. It is especially useful during high-stress situations, or during those times when you need to analyze your thoughts. By being able to detach yourself from your ideas and emotions, you can approach them with a more logical outlook. You can see where their flaws and points of improvement are. You are less likely to use them as an excuse to react rashly. Successfully attaining a passive mind at will can be a great asset for your daily life, with countless applications. Once you can achieve the passive state of mind at will, it's time to move on to more advanced meditative practices.

Third Eye Visualization Meditation

This exercise builds upon passive mind meditation and incorporates visualization techniques designed to prepare the third eye for activation. Follow these steps thoroughly:

- Sit comfortably in your meditation area. Make sure everything is quiet around you. Make sure you're also wearing comfortable clothing, as you may find yourself sweating after this meditation. This is natural as your body detoxifies and reacts to the new sensations.

- Enter the passive state of your mind, as you have done before. As you do, try to "spill" all the thoughts of your mind in front of you—every thought currently in your mind should be represented in your field of thought. Keep all the thoughts within "reach," where you can gain easy access to them. As before, however, do not engage or indulge them.

- In your mind, stretch out your hand and "push" the thoughts away. It should be a gentle pushing motion, as you visualize the thoughts growing farther and farther away. Let the momentum of the push carry your thoughts farther and farther until they disappear into the horizon.

- Repeat this process so long as new thoughts pop up. In the end, you should be alone with your thoughts in the field.

- Now that you are alone, visualize a glowing white orb forming around you. This is an orb of gentle white light, occupying the space where your thoughts once were.

- Visualize this globe of light slowly, smoothly contracting towards your head. In the end, the globe should just be a small speck of intense white light, nestled against where your pineal gland would be (in the middle of your head, back from the point of your forehead between the two eyebrows).

- As you do this, the light from the orb should wash everything around you in a gentle white light. Visualize this light slowly rotating, in the center of your head. You should feel calm and content, empty of all thoughts. You may also feel a certain buzzing in your head, reverberating throughout your body as the pinpoint of light in your head spins.

- As you meditate on the ball of light in your Ajna chakra, feel its light slowly growing brighter, encompassing your whole body. As it does, feel yourself becoming lighter and lighter. Let the calmness radiate around you, as you feel everything becomes still. Rise through this stillness, as if even gravity itself has ceased to weigh you down.

- As you float up, let the light from your forehead stream out in front of you. At this point, open yourself to the thoughts of your mind. Let the thoughts swimming around in front of you again, as they did before when you were still back on the ground. Note that these thoughts may not be the usual thoughts you are accustomed to. Sometimes these thoughts are completely alien—note that at this point, you are starting to get glimpses of that part of your mind that is locked away from conscious thought. Your Ajna chakra is starting to respond, and you are getting a sneak peek into the wonders it could reveal.

Chapter 22
Third Eye Activation

For many years, humankind has believed in the concept of the third eye. Representation of the third eye and the pinecone, which is a symbol of the pineal gland, can be witnessed almost everywhere. The Egyptians believed in the concept. Hindus and Buddhists still firmly believe in the concept of the third eye. We revered the third eye so much because we knew that it could unlock several amazing abilities. Apart from knowledge, wisdom, and intellect, the third eye also can unlock psychic abilities. When your third eye has awakened, you look at the world with a better vision. You have an all-seeing eye inside you that can help you in witnessing things that others can't. This is a reason most people intrigued by the occult and amazing phenomena are mesmerized by the idea of the third eye. You can have some of these abilities if you have awakened your third eye.

Clairvoyance (Psychic Visions)

It is the ability of psychic sight. This means that you can see what others can't. People have always considered this ability a gift. However, we all have this ability to some extent. Some young children have stronger clairvoyant abilities than adults. They can sense spirits, energies, and future mishaps. Their minds are not fully developed to understand the meanings of some signals, but they do see things more clearly. As we age, our pineal gland gets calcified and our psychic abilities become dim. The third eye activation also involves decalcification of the pineal gland. It helps in improving our sense of perception. We can sense the presence of energies, spirits, and omens better. As our minds are more mature, we may be able to deduce the correct meanings of those signals. This is among the most desired psychic abilities of all as it gives you a real hold of the things happening around you. You can even predict things that haven't even happened yet with some level of accuracy. This doesn't happen due to magic. Your mind can feel the energies. Your body in itself is an intense ball of energy. When your sense of perception increases due to third eye awakening, you can feel these energies clearly. This heightened sense of perception makes you stand apart from others. You can develop clairvoyant abilities by practicing meditation once your third eye has been activated.

Observing Auras

This whole universe is a form of energy. We, being a part of the universe, are also energy. The characteristic quality of energy is that it radiates itself. Every living being has an electromagnetic field of energy engulfing the whole persona. This field of energy is called the aura. Our body is simply not just the physical form. Emotional, etheric, mental, astral, celestial energies are also present in the body. All these energies emit specific radiations or auras in form of colors. These colors can be seen, and they can help in identifying the kind of energy that dominates a person. This art is called observing auras. When your third eye becomes active and starts functioning properly, you can develop the powers to see these auras or energy fields. Most of us have this power, but it is never very strong. Yet, when you go to someplace or meet someone you can feel the negative energy or vibe coming. You don't need the help of others to tell you this. Third eye awakening simply magnifies this ability several times. You will be able to clearly distinguish auras without opening your eyes. You will be able to feel auras that don't even have a physical body. You will be able to see energy, dark or light in its most vivid form. This ability starts developing naturally when you meditate and activate your third eye. You will be able to feel the presence of negative or positive energies. The vibes coming from people will be very clear and strong. You wouldn't need an introduction to know the basic traits of a person. If you want to develop this ability, then meditation and focus are the main ways to do so.

Astral Projection or Astral Travel

Astral Projection is a way to have out-of-body experiences. This is, again, an ability that we all have to some extent. At times of near-death experiences, traumas, illnesses, people may feel like they have left the body and traveled far. However, such experiences are never voluntary. 'Dreaming while awake' will be a better description of astral travel. We are made up of energies. With the psychic abilities provided by the third eye, you can make your energies leave your body and travel at will. Although astral travels last for brief periods, your experience can be very, very long, because as in other dimensions, time is not relative. You can communicate with other energies that do not hold a body of their own. You can travel far away and return. You remain in complete control of yourself. You will be able to see the world from a completely different perspective. Your view of the world would completely change.

Although the projection looks very mystical, it is a reality. We all are not just this body. This body is a very insignificant part of our actual being. We won't simply die when this body stops functioning. On the levels of energy, we will continue to live forever. You can develop the powers of astral projection by awakening your third eye and making it powerful by doing meditation regularly. All these powers are real; we have all of them in dormant forms as we do not exercise them regularly. You can make them stronger by practicing them regularly.

However, it is important that before you start to practice these powers, you strengthen your powers fully. All energies around us are not positive and harmless. The world is full of negative energies and they will try to interact with you or influence you. If you do not have enough protection, you may be influenced by them and bring harm to yourself. Meditation is one of the best ways to activate your third eye and strengthen its powers. You will be able to develop the desired powers with meditation and keep them in your control. If you remain dedicated and focused, there is nothing that will stop you from achieving your goals.

How to Activate the Third Eye by Breathing

It is essential first to know the location of what you are trying to activate. The third eye is found in between the face skull and brain. It is essential to access the third eye so that it then becomes more comfortable for you to activate it. The way to get yourself there is by focusing your mind on that said location, eyes closed and relaxed, and with a relaxed face as well. The head should be let loose such that there are no tensed head muscles. Let loose everything by allowing the head and face risk so that your only focus will be the area where the third eye resides. You might likely get distracted, but there is a way around this, and that would be by trying to get your images together. Imagining a specific thing or spot where you will put all your imagination is essential. You could visualize a small dot and put all your thoughts on the dot, try very hard to ensure that you concentrate on that space. At that time of your concentration, do not allow any other thoughts to take you away from your point of focus. When you have been able to gather all your thoughts at that particular spot, you are now ready to focus even with your eyes wide open. When you feel that you are totally comfortable and that you are now in contact with your third eye, you may start to increase your visualization. Start slowly, as you go up, do not pressure yourself to reach the peak when you are not ready. Take your time to visualize whatever it is you want to deal with, do not be afraid if the process is taking too much time, and be gradual but sure. It is essential not to forget to let loose. Relax with every level of visualization; being tense will only distract you further. Try reaching the third eye with your eyes open imagining the process, the journey, and how you actually feel connecting with it. The mind is also found in the third area location and helps the eyes and the brain to relax. When you have relaxed the eyes and the brain, the third eye then becomes stronger and much clear to understand. This process is also the process that we use to let in the warmth from the sun to get into our body system and freshen up the entire body give us new energy levels. If the process feels uncomfortable and even starts to hurt your head, it's good to relax or let go and you can always do it another time when you are more relaxed. People usually make the mistake of trying to lift their eyeballs as if they want to see the third eye while still in visualization. The right way to go about this is by letting the eyeballs relax as well; let them stay in their normal place. Let the eyeballs rest in their sockets and still try to focus on your visualization of the third eye. However, let the neck go a little higher by lifting your head a little high. When you are sure you are in this position, take a deep breath, relax the face, neck, and shoulders. Resting the eyes is one of the small challenges you have to experience in the process so that you know if you are doing it right. Copy the movement made by the sun as it sets because in doing so, your eyes will automatically relax. When you are at a point where you can relax your body muscles, you will begin to grasp an unexplained understanding. The exercise is very important as it acts as a connector between a person, the heavens, and even the earth.

Having the Third Eye Experience

Activating the third eye should not be a quick process. It should be a gradual process where you do not put any pressure on yourself, inhale and allow yourself time. Taking the time to relax is an excellent way to achieve the visualization needed in the third eye. If you cannot find yourself relaxing naturally, take time off before starting the meditation process. During that break, allow yourself to prepare for the meditation you are about to do mentally. Let your mind feel the energy to go through so that when you begin, it becomes easier. This will help create awareness to the third eye of what is about to happen and the third eye, on the other hand, will provide clarity. Reopening the third eye should not be a forced process, it should come out naturally and that is why one is encouraged to take their time. The process takes a lot of years of training; it doesn't just happen in a day.

Chapter 23
Lucid Dreams: What Are and How to Experience Them

Lucid dreams are where the dreamer is aware of dreaming. In the lucid dream, the person is already outside their body. Lucid dreams—also known as becoming conscious during the dream state—are among the most interesting states of sleep. The dreams are so vivid that you experience real emotions while awake in a dream state and many people even feel that certain events in these dreams will come true in their waking lives. Lucidity in dreams is a state that most dreamers have experienced from time to time. You can't control the outcome of events while you are conscious of a dream. If you can make yourself lucid in dreams, on the other hand, you can rewrite the dream and make it go any way you want. You will have full control of your actions and experiences by reinterpreting the dream as you are conscious of it. Lucidity in dreams is a state that many people experience at some time or another. These people are actually experiencing a form of lucid dreaming without knowing it for most of the time, just like I am right now.

The term "lucid dreaming" is a new word to describe those experiences. The true definition of lucid dreaming is the ability to become consciously aware during the dream state. You can then control your actions in dreams and rewrite what is happening. If you can obtain this ability, you will be able to perform magical feats that even Harry Potter could not accomplish, such as controlling your destiny and becoming the hero of your own story. However, true lucid dreaming is still a rare occurrence. Most people experience it only once every so often and never learn to have full control over their sleeping selves. The reason stems from our inability to keep our minds awake while we are dreaming. You can't consciously control something when you are asleep. If you want to make an important decision during your dream state, you won't be able to do it. You will be lodged in a circle of events that will never change. Lucid dreams are a form of spatial awareness in sleep that can help you achieve great things in waking life. They allow you to visualize the things that you want to happen in your life and prepare for the future. One of the most useful benefits of lucid dreaming is the ability to rehearse important events in your life. If you have a crucial performance coming up, you can visualize yourself doing it perfectly every time before the real event occurs. When you become conscious in dreams but still remain asleep, you learn how to relax and get rid of all stress and anxiety before an important event occurs. This will then allow you to feel refreshed and confident on the day of the actual event. Another very important use of lucid dreaming is the ability to travel to places around the world. You can start with your dream home, move to any place you like, and explore all that is around you. When you are fully lucid in dreams, you have a full awareness of all things around you. In this way, you can create vivid dreams and places that will allow you to explore new worlds and visit them before waking up for real life. The benefits of lucid dreams are many. Make certain that you comprehend each one before you begin your training and develop your own ways to use them in the future. Learn how to control your thoughts and actions, and you can rewrite anything that happens in a dream. This awareness will help you become successful in all areas of life, giving you new tools to visualize both the future and the past. Lucid dreams are usually caused by stress or exhaustion. The main cause of this particular state of consciousness is the presence of high amounts of carbon dioxide in your blood. This stimulant causes the brain to release chemicals such as adrenaline and serotonin, which result in a short burst of energy. This state of mind is also caused by a high number of sleep-related hormones in your body. Dopamine, for example, often causes vivid and intense dreams when it builds up during sleep. If you cannot fall asleep because of anxiety, you will be more prone to having lucid dreams. The key to achieving lucid dreaming is to learn how to remain conscious in your dreams without becoming fully awake and aware of your surroundings. Learn how to focus on one thing at a time so that only that specific idea or memory remains. This prevents you from becoming fully awake. The trick is to learn how to remain conscious throughout the dream and have your sleeping self focus on a single image or thought that can trigger your lucidity. Become obsessed with out-of-body experiences, and you desire it. It's important that you read as much about it as you can. You need to think about it constantly. When your mind is ridden with thoughts of out-of-body experiences, you need affirmations and triggers so you can have lucid dreams. All-day long think about having a lucid dream.

The Reality Tests

Ask yourself if you are dreaming now. You will have the capacity to program your subconscious to make a lucid dream possible. Once you're in one of these dreams, and you aware of it, begin to notice that you are no longer in your body. You will be able to make yourself to see your bedroom. When you do this, your dream world will disappear, and you will find yourself floating about your body. Practice this every day and observe what happens in your life. This helps you to have memories to use in lucid dreams.

Use guided Meditation Daily

These meditations are useful because they help you calm down and focus your mind while sleeping. You can also use these meditations to focus on a certain topic while in dreams. See below for guided meditation tips.

Practice Dream Recall

While this might seem simple, it actually has a lot of benefits that make it worth practicing every day. It helps you stay conscious of your dreams when you wake up, and it allows you to be more relaxed and aware of all things around you. While this might seem simple, it has a lot of benefits that make it worth practicing every day. It helps you stay conscious of your dreams when you wake up, and it allows you to be more relaxed and aware of all things around you. Get enough sleep. You will need a lot of sleep to achieve lucid dreaming. This is correct for all, but especially if you want to have lucid dreams regularly. Make sure that your sleep is natural and restful. If you can fall asleep quickly and stay asleep for a long time, your chances of having a lucid dream increase as well.

Guided Meditations for Lucid Dreams

If you are interested in using guided meditations to have lucid dreams, here is a guide with some of the best meditations and how to use them:

1. Progressive muscle relaxation. You will need to do 1-minute of relaxation for each body part you want to relax. This meditation will help you get back into the habit of sleeping deeply and getting enough sleep every night. If you are unable to get enough sleep every night, try this meditation to give your body the rest it needs.

2. Breathwork. This is another excellent guided meditation that helps you get deeper into sleep and relax your mind. You will need to breathe in and out deeply for 20 seconds and then try again for another 20 seconds.

3. Affirmations. This is a different guided meditation because it will help you focus on achieving a lucid dream. You will need to repeat an affirmation for 10 minutes at night and think of a specific object or situation you want to encounter in your dreams.

Here are some suggestions for affirmations:

- "I'm dreaming"—This can be useful if you are not sure if you are dreaming or not. You can ask yourself, "Am I dreaming?" and you will be able to answer the question before looking at your surroundings.

- "I will lucid dream tonight"—This type of affirmation is more helpful for people that rarely have lucid dreams or have trouble having them. By repeating this affirmation 10 minutes before you go to sleep, you will achieve a lucid dream without much effort.

4. Crystal ball. This is another great guided meditation for achieving a lucid dream. You can either say the words yourself or listen to someone else saying them. It is a little bit more complicated but many people have had success with this method.

5. Binaural Beats. This is another guide that will help you achieve lucid dreams. It is simpler than the crystal ball method but it will still help you get there easier and faster than you normally would, especially if you are new to lucid dreaming.

6. Mindfulness Meditation. This is another guided meditation for lucid dreaming. However, this is a real meditation so it will help you relax and stay relaxed all throughout the day. It is great to listen to before going to sleep as well.

7. Brainwave Entrainment. This method of achieving lucid dreams can be achieved by listening to binaural beats created exclusively for that purpose, or you can make some yourself using an app like Binaural Beats Meditation. You can create the sound in your desired frequency and listen through headphones if you wish; a stereo headphone jack will allow you to choose which ear corresponds with the beat frequency. With binaural beats, your brain responds by creating its sound wave, which is subsequently sent to your ears. Your brain does this because it associates these two tones with what's happening in your environment. The result is that you hear a third tone, between those two original frequencies.

8. Agni Fire Meditation. This guided meditation is great for inducing lucid dreams. You can use it once per day for 20 minutes and you will begin to notice a difference in no time at all—your dreams will begin to be much more vivid and intense, even if you are not focused on a particular topic while sleeping.

9. Brainwave Generator. This is an online tool that will allow you to create your brainwaves so that you can use them as background sound to help induce lucid dreams. You will need to get this tool if you are interested in doing this.

10. Subliminal messages. A subliminal message is a message that is part of your unconscious mind and can be heard by your conscious mind. This means that you will be able to hear it when you are not aware of it, which is why it can be so effective for lucid dreaming.

Chapter 24
Astral Projection for Beginners

The very idea that humans can exit their bodies while sleeping is ancient. Countless people believe it is possible to communicate with cosmic beings through vivid dreams and visions that are experienced by astral travel.

Between eight and twenty percent of people say they have had something similar to an out-of-body experience at one point in their lives. A sensation that their consciousness, or spirit is leaving their body. Many experience this during sleep or while hypnotized; some can do it while just relaxing. The astral plane is one in the fifth dimension. This is where dreams take place. Where magical teachings are provided and where the dead go. You might get lucky enough to meet spiritual beings there. You can discover what happens when you die, your purpose in life, receive guidance, have premonitions about your future, have an awakening, learn wisdom about death, learn your inner defects, see your spiritual obstacles, learn what you don't know about yourself, and discover secret knowledge. You will find yourself in another world that exists outside this world. You can fly, walk through objects and walls, meet new people, and travel to distant lands. It is a wonderful experience. The reality is made by thoughts projecting consciousness into the physical realm. When your astral project, the conscious mind will leave the physical body and move into the astral body for the experience. You stay attached to your physical self through a silver cord. Some might see this cord when they astral project. To be able to astral project, you must feel completely relaxed, wear comfortable clothing, and be lying down. Put a comforter over you since the physical body might get cold when your spirit travels out of it. You will stay aware of everything you experienced when you were not in your physical body. Some people can do this easily, while some are a little afraid to remove their consciousness from the physical body, so they choose not to learn. Astral travel can be achieved either awake or through deep meditation or lucid dreaming. People who have experienced astral projection say their spirit left their physical body and moved into the spirit world. This concept dates back to ancient China and has been around for thousands of years. Psychics say the mind that dreams hold the astral body and this causes sudden jerks that wake you up or falling dreams. Many dreams aren't remembered and thus cause astral travel to be a subject of individuality. Those who believe in astral travel will often mention those ghost sightings are typically described as transparent apparitions that walking the earth.

It isn't clear if every object has an astral counterpart or if the spirit just incarnates into a body, and this results in astral travel. The phenomena might be something entirely different. Astral travel deals a little with life and the things that happen after death. There are two different thoughts on the nature of astral travel. A broad definition of these would be a phasing model and a mystical model. The phasing model believes that it's possible to leave your body. The astral plane and the physical world are both areas of our conscious spectrum. When someone chooses to project, they are phasing into a different area of consciousness and the locations there. You can compare this to changing the radio station. This viewpoint is seen as the external reality is only a state that is created internally. The mystical model has many astral maps and belief systems but is connected to the belief that astral travel happens outside the physical body. An energy body is thought to carry the consciousness out of the physical body. Higher planes are reached by progressive projections of subtle energy bodies from other projected bodies. This body is connected to the physical one through an energetic connection that looks like a silver cord some refer to as an umbilical cord.

There are hundreds possibly thousands of techniques to help your astral travel. Everybody is different, so something that works for one may not work for another. Try one and if it doesn't work for you, move to a different one.

The Rope Technique

The main object in this technique is to picture a rope hanging off the ceiling. The point of this rope is to provide pressure at a certain area on the astral body so that it will separate itself from your physical one.

1. Reach out with your imagined hands and pull on yourself. Get yourself hand over hand up the rope that is above you. You may experience dizziness. This sensation will become stronger the farther up the rope you go.

2. Continue to climb and you will start to feel the vibration. Your entire body will feel like it is vibrating and you may end up feeling paralyzed. Focus completely on the climb and don't stop.

3. This is where you feel yourself being freed from your body. Your astral body will leave the physical in the rope's direction. You will now notice that you are hovering above your body. Now you are free.

Watch Yourself Sleep

1. Lie down and make sure you're comfortable on your back, look towards the ceiling. Completely relax and allow your mind to let go of unwanted thoughts.

2. Let yourself know that you are going to watch yourself fall asleep. You will have to be clear about your intentions. Let the body sleep while your mind stays alert. Tell yourself to keep consciousness while your body is going into a trance.

3. Once you completely relax, you will need to become familiar with the sensations that your body has as you fall asleep. You need to be aware while this happens. You will feel your body feels numb and heavy.

4. Pay attention to your body's sensations. You might sense like you are rising above or swaying. You might feel tingling sensations in certain areas. You could even feel vibrations surging through your entire body. You may even have buzzing in your ears. Whatever you feel, don't panic as these are signals that you are on the right path.

5. You need to visualize you are rising from your bed and float to the ceiling. How will it feel if you did float? Make this experience as real as you can. Hold this image. If everything works, you will notice that you are floating above your body.

The Monroe Technique

1. An important part of this is that you completely relax.

2. Now try to get yourself to go to sleep without falling asleep. Keep an awareness of being between awake and asleep. This is what they refer to as a hypnagogic state. Let this state deepen and release all of your bad thoughts.

3. Now peer through your eyelids into the blackness.

4. Now relax deeper. Bring vibrations into your body and make them become more intense. You need to continue to control and grow these more. During this time is when the astral body will leave your physical body. Then roll yourself over, and you will see the physical body below you.

Displaced Awareness Technique

1. Shut your eyes and let yourself enter a trance state. Notice your room. Feel yourself about your shoulders and see all around. Don't acknowledge anything directly.

2. Now picture the astral body rotating. When you have finished the mental rotation, your astral head will be where your physical feet are. The astral feet should be where the physical head is positioned. Now that you have this, picture the room from this perspective.

3. Let go of where you are located and get rid of your sense of direction. When this is done correctly, you will feel dizzy. This is what you want.

4. When you're comfortable, imagine floating toward the ceiling. Make this feel as real as you can. During this, you will suddenly find that you have left your physical body.

The Jump Technique

When this technique is performed correctly, you will awaken from your dreams, and they will become lucid. This has to be done well.

1. Ask yourself repeatedly throughout the day if you're dreaming or not. It is important to do this because you need to know where you are.
2. You have to make yourself doubt that you are in the physical world.
3. For proof, jump just like you are flying. If you are really in your physical body, your feet will hit the ground. If you're in a dream when you jump, you will begin to float.

After a few days of this, you will notice that you start to jump into your dreams to see whether or not you are dreaming. When you jump, you will be floating.

The Stretch Out Technique

1. Lay down, close your eyes, and relax.
2. Imagine your feet stretching and getting longer by an inch or so. When you have this in your mind, let your feet shrink back to normal.
3. Repeat with the head.
4. Now alternate between your feet and head until they stretch about two feet. Now stretch them together. This starts the vibrations and will cause you to feel dizzy.

Whichever one of these techniques you pick, you will not see any results the first time, or even the first couple of times. Take it slowly, and don't become frustrated when things don't happen. You will begin to see some results with time. You might have a physical or mental block that is preventing you from getting out of your body. You may have some past trauma, a bad diet, or an unhealthy pineal gland that you need to deal with. It could be a lot of different things. Don't worry if you don't remember any details about your astral travels. You must write them down after you have finished your travel. When you are half asleep, everything seems obvious, and you think you will remember it forever. You might be so comfortable you want to fall asleep. Stand up and write down the details, you can reconstruct the information later. The important thing here is not what you do but why you do it. This applies to your thoughts. Just think about it. You need to be completely honest with yourself. Cleanse your mind from all garbage and never follow the flock.

How far can you go in this universe? There are no limits.

Chandra Wilbur

Chapter 25
The Facets of Awakening

The Facet of Mind

Seekers awakening to this facet gradually or suddenly become aware of their conditioning and see its influence on their beliefs and views of the world around them. This mental programming dissolves in the mind of the seeker and is replaced with consciousness, and there are no longer any emotional or mental concepts that can surprise or fool the seeker.

Our un-awakened human sense of self is strongly linked with our feelings and emotions. If we are angry, we say that "I" am angry. If we feel sad, we link our self with that single emotion. To awaken to emotion means that the seeker no longer defines their sense of self from how they feel. They understand very deeply that emotions are only a product of the brain and have no permanence or ability to affect a person's thoughts or behavior.

Awakening to the facet of the mind also uncovers the difference between thinking and awareness. The seeker is no longer fooled by the products of the brain and becomes aware that their thinking and feeling are separate from their awareness or consciousness. For instance, after fully awakening to the mind, the Seeker can watch feelings and emotions in their mind without being drawn into them and can observe the feelings and emotions from their beginning all the way through their entire life cycle to their complete and total end, without letting their judgment be affected by them.

At this stage, the Seeker also becomes aware of the ego and its function in the human mind. However, it must be pointed out that most Seekers will not understand the entire range and size of their ego until they fully awaken to the facet of self.

For most, awakening to the mind represents a revolutionary transformation. One no longer defines oneself through what one feels. This doesn't mean that the Awakened person does not have feelings or emotions; the body and the mind still create anger, hate, jealousy, greed, lust, and guilt, etc., but rather than influencing the judgment of the person, it is the person that decides what impact, if any, their feelings and emotions should have in any life situation.

To the fully Awakened person, all emotions become highly useful tools that can help them to become aware of unsolved wounds or traumas within themselves, or that they may be falling back to past conditioning.

The Facet of Self

Seekers awakening to this facet gradually or suddenly become aware of their ego in its totality, which was seen and thoroughly understood by Buddhism several thousand years ago, and modern science is only now catching up.

When a seeker can see past their ego and all of their attachments fall away, they can separate thinking and awareness, and with that, the awakened person completely ceases to suffer altogether, in that they completely and permanently enter a state of mind of total and complete acceptance to all that is, the present moment, without choosing between moments or preferring one moment over another.

The now awakened person can truly take responsibility for their entire life and everything that has happened in it. They no longer blame others for their past suffering, understanding now that suffering is a product of the ego. The awakened person no longer tries to force their thinking on any other person, understanding that everyone is already making the best decisions that they can in the present moment and that we all are responsible for our learning and inner growth.

After integrating these new understandings into daily life, the seeker usually loses all concern with forms (emotional, physical, and thought). They become confident and a deep and powerful sense of self-worth blooms into permanent existence. Their need for the old style of relationships changes and they no longer desire to fit in or be "normal," and they allow themselves to be exactly who they are without the need for approval or acceptance from anyone.

The awakened seeker's personality may undergo a shift that may be noticeable to those around them to varying degrees. A common misunderstanding here is that an awakened person's personality changes upon awakening or enlightenment, but this is not accurate. A person that has fully awakened to the facet of self will have the same personality after as before, minus any character or personality traits that were not wholesome or did not move the person along the path to spiritual enlightenment.

Gone is the desire to, or automatic habit of, fitting into "normal" society, or of being politically correct, or yielding to authority. Rather, the seeker now makes decisions based on what is best for themselves and for all others involved in any situation, rather than what their ego wants. Constantly chasing happiness ends as the seeker now understands that nothing outside of themselves can make them happy.

The Facet of Spiritual Energy

Basically speaking, spiritual energy is universal energy that flows into and through the human body through various points. When a seeker awakens to the existence of spiritual energy, which is also known as qi, prana, chakras, or kundalini energy, changes will occur on the physical, mental and spiritual levels. Ancient practices such as Tai Chi, yoga, meditation, and tantra can help to awaken this energy, which can happen gradually or all at once, just like any other awakening.

The Facet of Universal Consciousness

Universal Consciousness comes from the source of all life, which some refer to as cosmic intelligence, the Source, God, Allah, the Great Spirit, and so forth. Human Consciousness comes from Universal Consciousness, and so one can never be separate from it, but humans do not know this until they awaken. Universal Consciousness exists across the entire cosmos, or all of space and time, though Universal Consciousness exists outside of time and space. Perhaps it can best be described as the unknowable intelligence behind and guiding the evolution of what humans view as the physical universe.

When Awakening to Universal Consciousness, either gradually over time or in a great explosion from within, Human Consciousness expands to touch the whole world and to even touch the stars. A seeker gains a new understanding of the nature of reality and may feel an infusion of love or wisdom. If they have not done so as the result of awakening to another facet, duality concepts such as good and bad dissolve completely, and the Seeker understands that inside every person, every tree, every rock, every planet, every galaxy, every particle of light and every moment in time is simply pure love.

Seekers who awaken fully to this facet understand that there is no meaning or purpose to life itself. Love for life and everyone and everything in it springs from within the heart of the Seeker, and they find great happiness in their reconnection to everyone and everything.

If they have not already, a seeker will lose all fear of death at this stage, and their sole focus becomes living in the present moment. When human consciousness is seen as surviving the physical body, fear of the loss of the body ceases to be a constant worry. Time and distance go back to simply being human concepts as the seeker understands that they are just ways of thinking to help humans measure change and relative physical location.

Lastly, the seeker is filled with the comprehension that the entire universe is connected and that trees, plants, rocks, the human body, planets, and stars all consist of the same material, and all material originally came from the same place.

The Source, or God.

The Facet of True Reality

"Seeing is believing" is one of those sayings that support what is perhaps the biggest of all the things that humans have misunderstood at one point or another, that our reality around us is exactly and only what we see through our eyes.

But it is not. Not even close.

Science tells us that the human eye can only see 0.005% of existing energy waves called "visible light." This means that 99.995% of light is not visible to the human eye. Astronomers and astrophysicists estimate that only 4% of the universe is viewable to the naked eye or any other current technology, the other 96% thought to be "dark matter" or "dark energy" that is not yet detectable.

Also consider the basic building block for everything in our universe, the atom. It is generally accepted that our universe is about fourteen billion years old, though some theories place the age at much older than that. All of the carbon, nitrogen, and oxygen atoms in our galaxy, in our solar system, on this planet, and in our bodies were created in stars older than our sun.

The facets of Awakening can be developed in any order, speed, or level relative to each other. Being awake to one facet may help awaken the Seeker to another facet, while other facets have no relation at all.

Chapter 26
Learn More About the Chakras

The Base or Root Chakra

The first chakra we will discover is the root or the base chakra. When you are engaging in this chakra, you will be concentrating on the color red and the place is going to be right at the bottom of your spinal cord. It is also about your privilege to exist. It can also function with your capacity to hold up for yourself and most of the time it will identify your safety issues.

When this chakra is not functioning effectively, there can be several various health problems that you have to work on. You may discover that you will endure from unwarm hands and freezing feet as well as common colds. There can also be problems with anxiety, sciatica, lower back pain, lethargy, and even anemia.

If you would like to arouse this specific chakra, you would have to make certain that you are keeping your body well taken care of with several restful sleep and exercise. In addition, things that aid you to get nearer to the earth, such as pottery, working with clay, and gardening, can aid you to feel good.

Spleen Chakra

When you are working with the spleen chakra, you will notice that you are working with the chakra that is going to focus on the color orange. This is the one that is found near the lower abdomen and slightly below the navel. This is chakra affects your feelings. It is connected with how well you can sense what is going on with other people and it is going to show some of your issues with feelings when it isn't its proper working order. It also is in charge of how social and intimate you can be with other people.

When this particular chakra is not working there can be a wide variety of issues that show up. This one is going to be associated with some eating disorders as well as abuse of drugs and alcohol. It can also be associated with frigidity, impotency, urinary problems, yeast infections, asthma, back pain, in the lower back, depression, and more.

Some water aerobics and hot baths with essential oils work really well on this one. Doing a message is also good. You will want to concentrate on working with the sensations in your life to stimulate this particular chakra. Of course, anything with orange is going to work well with this chakra, such as orange oils, orange clothing and gemstones, and even orange drinks and food.

Solar Plexus Chakra

Another great chakra that you can focus on is the solar plexus chakra. This one is going to be associated with the color yellow, so you will want to concentrate on this color if you want to make your solar plexus chakra better. This one is going to be found in the stomach area as well, but it is above the navel and therefore, a bit higher up. This chakra is all about your own personal power and your right to think. It is also about balancing ego power, self-confidence, and intellect. It can also be important in helping you to have some self-control as well as a sense of humor in everyday life. When the solar plexus chakra is not effectively working, you will notice that there are a lot of issues that come with the stomach area. Some of the issues that can come up when this one is imbalanced include poor memory, colitis, parasites, toxicity, nervousness, constipation, diabetes, ulcers, and digestive problems. It is essential to prioritize the solar plexus chakra. You can do this by working on things that will help to build up your mind and will ensure that you are feeling your best with your self-confidence. This would include things like doing mind puzzles, reading books to help you learn, and taking classes. Spending time outside can help with this as well. Using yellow foods and drinks as well as sticking to yellow oils, clothing, and gemstones can help to work with the solar plexus chakra.

The Heart Chakra

This one is associated with the green color, so you will need to concentrate on this color as you go along. The heart chakra is all about your right to love and is all about relationships. It is about compassion, forgiveness, and love. It is also for acceptance of yourself and the ability to have some self-control in your life. When the heart chakra is not functioning effectively, it is going to cause many problems. With this one, you may notice that there can be an issue of breast and heart cancer, as well as chest pain. There are often the heart and other breathing disorders that occur when the heart chakra is not working the way that it should. High blood pressure, muscular tension, immune system problems, and even issues with passivity will occur when this particular chakra is not working the way that it should. If you would like to work on this particular type of chakra, there are several things that you can do to help it feel better. Going out and spending some time with family and friends as much as you can and spending some time out in nature, such as going for a nature walk can help to make it better. Sticking with things that are green, such as green essential oils, green clothing, and gemstones, and even green foods can help.

The Throat Chakra

The throat chakra is another one that you will need to focus on a bit if you would like to help get your chakras lined up the right way. This is the chakra that will be associated with the color blue and you will be able to find it right in the region of the throat. This is another one that is going to deal with relationships as well, but it is more focused on your right to speak. This is one about learning how to express yourself and how to express your beliefs. It is the speaking chakra, but it is the one that is concerned with speaking the truth while speaking up for oneself. It is also about planning and organization, as well as loyalty and your ability to trust. When this one is imbalanced, you may see that there are quite a few different things that are wrong with your life. You can have issues with your shoulders, neck, tongue, jaw, and mouth and it is common to have an imbalance in your thyroid. Some hormonal disorders, such as menopause, bloating, mood swings, and even PMS can be associated with this chakra not doing the work that it should. Singing, such as singing in the shower, works great as do meaningful conversations, poetry, and more. This chakra is connected with the color blue, so you will want to concentrate on blue food and drinks, blue oils and clothing, and so on.

Third Eye Chakra

The next chakra on the list is known as the brow chakra or the third eye chakra. You will be able to find this one on the forehead, usually right between the eyes. When you are looking at this chakra, you will notice that it is the color indigo. This is the chakra that is linked with your intuition and that gut feeling that you have sometimes. It is all about trusting your insights and intuition and can help you develop your psychic abilities, provided you learn how to use them in the right way. Releasing some of those hidden, as well as repressed negative thoughts and learning about your self-realization can be achieved with this third eye chakra. When the third eye chakra is not working the proper way or it isn't balanced, you will notice that a lot of the same issues as the throat chakra, in terms of mood disorders or with the thyroid being imbalanced will be seen. In addition, there are a few other issues that can come up when the third eye chakra is not working properly such as sleep disorders, coordination problems, and even learning disabilities. If you would like to make sure that your third eye chakra is working right and you can work with your intuition more, there are a few options that you can work with, such as meditation and stargazing. You can also concentrate on the color indigo in your drink and food as well as the essential oils, clothing, and more that you choose to work with.

The Crown Chakra

And finally, it is time to work on the crown chakra. This is the chakra that is going to be associated with the violet color. When you are dealing with this chakra, it is all about knowingness and the right to aspire. It is all about connecting your physical body with the universe and your spiritual world. It is a great chakra to use when you want to learn about the spirituality of yourself and it is like your connection to a higher power. This can be a really hard one for a lot of people to concentrate on when they are busy always worrying about things of the physical world.

When the crown chakra is not working properly, you are going to have a lot of issues that come with your mental wellbeing. This one can cause issues like senility, neuralgia, mental illness, headaches, and even issues with your coordination, as well as left and right brain disorders. Sometimes there are going to be some issues that come with skin rashes, blood vessel problems, and epilepsy if you don't take care of this chakra as you should.

You can start by focusing on what is going on in some of your dreams or even write down the visions and the different inventions that come to your head. Of course, you can also spend some of your time focusing on the color violet such as violet drinks, clothing, gemstones, and even some of the essential oils that are violet color, such as jasmine or lavender.

As you have learned, the chakras are all going to be connected with each other. When one of the chakras is not working the proper way, you are going to notice that this will affect the other chakras as well. If you don't take care of all of the chakras right from the beginning, you are slowly going to see the other chakras fail.

Understanding all of the chakras that you are working with is integral if you would like to see positive results. Each of the chakras is important and will spend some time helping to take care of the various parts of your body. When you can get them to line up properly, you are going to see some great results in the overall health and happiness of your body.

Chapter 27
Benefits of Reiki

Reiki draws its basis on a belief that there is a common and collective source of supernatural energy that brings about healing to our bodies. Masters are ever soliciting for this power to let it move through the body for healing to take place. Many are times when Reiki has been used by people on their own; however, it can be administered remotely from somebody else. It is also available in various health facilities but not limited to health clinics and hospitals. Recall that Reiki can be applied as a standalone therapy or in conjunction with other medicinal therapies. Reiki calls for someone's attention. When the Reiki session is ongoing, the client has to be silent and in a relaxed mode free from any physical movement.

Reiki was discovered very many years ago. It is a practical exercise and not theoretical. It entails the passing of signals to the client by putting hands closer to the client at specific body parts in intervals. It is a simple technique of linking somebody to the supernatural powers generally for a healing process to take place. The master or the practitioner has had prior training in the same procedure so that he can easily tap into the powers easily. He is how energy flows to the client. Whoever the client is, he has to infuse as much energy as possible to enable the body to be steady. A steady and balanced body can easily heal itself naturally.

Benefits of Reiki
Reiki just like any other natural healing procedure has very many advantages that are very unique as compared to other treatments. In fact, the advantages of Reiki outweigh any medical practice of healing that is administered to patients across the universe. These are very wonderful advantages of a very simple procedure yet with philosophical results.

Reiki Enhances Body Balance and Harmony

Reiki is effective in its way of operation. It is a profound mode of healing that supports the natural healing from invasions by leaving the body energized and feeling all well. Reiki lays its focus on bringing back the balance at every level as it directs the attention to the main challenge or condition. It is not limited to symptom relief.

Body balance is a very general term meaning the creation of equilibrium in our bodies. There is mental equilibrium, emotional equilibrium, female to male equilibrium, equilibrium of the brain, and perception of events as great or worse, appealing, or boring.

Reiki Acts as Stress and Tension Reliever from the Body

After a Reiki exercise, the body feels relaxed, deep enough that, even tension and any stress will vanish. Reiki gives people time for self-evaluation. They will have a good time for meditation as the treatment goes on. Meditation will allow clients to assess their own lives as they allow the life energy to run through their systems making them feel refreshed and relaxed; therefore, bringing about a sense of joy, and peace.

During a Reiki process, the clients stay calm. This helps them to detect whatever it is that goes around in their bodies, minds, and emotions. You have time to dialogue with your own body and therefore come up with possible solutions for the issues of life. This decision will make you much better than before.

Eliminates the Energy Blockages as It Enhances Equilibrium in the Body, Spirit, and Mind

All the blocks in the energy flow will be eliminated by frequent Reiki exercises. This creates a state of peace and a cool environment bringing down stress levels. When the mind is free, one can learn well and even have a good record of the events with a clear mind.

Emotional and mental wounds, when subjected to Reiki, will be healed easily. These are some of the factors that lead to frustrations, shifting in the mood graphs as well as changing anger patterns. They will all be cleared leaving the body much easy and in a healthier state. Relationships can also be restored and even become more powerful than they used to be as a result of the Reiki force. The fact that Reiki brings about love, after healing; it is love that will cause social cohesion between you and the people around you by creating great friendships and strong relationships.

Reiki Helps the Body in Self Purification Thus Promoting Immunity

There is much energy and time needed to fight stress and its causes that dictate the nature of lives. At long last, we forget to balance our lives. Our bodies are tuned to the game of stress management naturally until there is no room for relaxation. When Reiki comes in, it acts as a sympathizer that brings us to rest so that we can experience a moment of healing. At this state, you will still remain active as usual and much productive. The difference will be that your body will be given more room to rest and meditate which is essential for body health and strength. When you allow Reiki in your life, it makes the life more productive and active, free from stress and exhaustion or depletion.

Frees up the Mindset, Makes You More Focused, Rooted, and Stable

You will remain composed and in a steadier condition as opposed to, overthinking over the past events, or even worrying about the future unknowns. Reiki lets you live today as a day and not live in the past or the future. At the end of the day, you will feel sober even when the conditions are not favorable to you especially in your work environment. Instead of allowing the situations to control you, you will be in a position to challenge them and stand out as strong as if there was no challenge at all. You will end up being of great help to others who feel low or weak as a result of stress or de-motivation.

You Will Have Good and Enough Rest and Sleep

Healthy Sleep or rest comes as a result of a relaxed mindset. You can be able to sleep like a baby allowing your mind to meditate on good things, allow healing to take place more calmly, and even relate well with others. Reiki leads to sleep whenever you feel relieved of the pain and relaxed mind.

Reiki Promotes Own Healing the Moment You Attain a Self-Realization State

When you are sick or unwell, the state of the body will shift gears to begin imagining negativities. This creates a stressful mind and definitely weakens the body. It lowers your strength and therefore the power to overcome the symptoms generally goes down. This is a state we usually refer to as a compromised state. The immune system goes down as a result of the mindset and how it perceives the disease. There are many times when someone feels like; the current condition may lead to death. This is a compromised state that if not quickly dealt with, can cause an irreversible effect on someone's body through the mind. The healing of humanity begins with the mind. The mentality that this disease is incurable causes death. Reiki serves to deal with that condition hindering your mind from positive thinking to bring it back to normal so that you can see a possibility where there seems to be none. The healing power of Reiki seeks to reverse the order of events. It will lead you back to your original stable state hence allowing the body system to run in the correct route. Your blood pressure and pulse rate shall come back to normal. One aspect of the healing process is the ability to inhale and exhale deeper and freely. This leads to stability in our minds as proven scientifically. Our bodies were created to operate well in a balanced and stable mode rather than under tension and strife.

Works on Alleviating Unnecessary Body Pains Allowing the Healing of the Body Physically

We can describe Reiki as the healing power that works on humans in an outward-in motion. As we have seen before, the hands are put on the patient or the client on the outward but the feeling of the energy will be on the deep inside. The inside is arrived at via the outward. It is supernatural, so you do not need to question the procedure. It is naturally hard to reach the inside of a person except for a medical operation.

Therefore, Reiki is also a spiritual body surgery that does not involve the physical breaking of the body but through the spiritual flow of the energy from the outside to the inside. By putting your hand on the patients, it motivates the body to function in an improved way. That is a normal pulse, digestion, or even sleep.

Physically, some pains are associated with some illnesses which Reiki seeks to take away. For example, the pain associated with arthritis, headache or backache, and many more are just but a handful of the pains that you will be relieved from as you apply Reiki in your life.

Fosters Growth Spiritually and Emotional Purity

These are two concepts that work hand in hand. Your emotions and you're your spirit are key aspects that require attention else they can lead you into trouble. However, Reiki is independent of any spirituality in you. It can only be useful to anyone for improving your spiritual being even though its functionality is not dictated by the level of your spiritual growth. Reiki is a form of treatment that aids you in your personal healing expedition including your spiritual growth and development.

When administered, it touches the total life as opposed to drugs that target a specific area that require healing like a wound. It runs deep and searches deep into your system in a very unique way.

Reiki Is a Compliment of Medical Treatments

Very awesome is it for Reiki to serve as an addition to any other form of medication. Reiki is not physical and therefore it cannot be administered to patients as drugs for healing a specific illness. Neither is it a prescription by anyone to take away any form of disease across the globe. It is first of all voluntary and is believed to be spiritual. It, therefore, works hand in hand with other existing medical services offered to people or animals. This deals with soothing sorrows and wounds to bring about conditional healing rather than curing the disease itself. It both works on patient's minds and bodies. It is all about relaxation of the patient's minds as well as their bodies which in the long run spins the rate of healing. Sleep alone is a remedy to many anomalies. Reiki promotes nice sleep. Its sweetness is found in the way it is transferred. It is done very gently and in a persistent mode.

It Can Be Self-Taught

This is very good of Reiki practice. To get the knowledge of Reiki, you only need to attend the lessons for you to increase your levels of energy gradually on a day-to-day encounter. Many people opt for Reiki to help in their personal healing in many aspects.

Conclusion

Learning about spiritual awakening and its connection to other aspects can be overwhelming but it is so worth it. When you have the opportunity to understand it, you can apply it in reality to achieve the ultimate spiritual awakening.

The process of becoming self-aware and understanding your true nature as is in spiritual awakening can be a difficult journey for some people, but if you understand how to work the process, it can lead to greater happiness as you realize who you are. Regardless of your spiritual path or current beliefs, spiritual awakening may be worth taking the time to try out for yourself.

It's a process that some people experience and that others don't. It's often described as a state of blissful inner peace, where you feel complete and content daily. It can be both a physical sensation and a mental condition, where you feel more focused and clearer about your life with each passing day.

Here are some things to remember to achieve or even maintain spiritual awakening: Start by meditating every day. Another popular spiritual awakening technique is to start by sitting still for about 20 minutes a day, concentrating on your breathing and the sounds around you. It can help you find a feeling of calm, while also fostering your spiritual awakening process.

Embrace the present moment. The next step is to truly focus on what's going on around you. Be aware of the sounds around you, the temperature in the room, or how your body feels at that very moment. Stop worrying about the past or future. The next step in your spiritual awakening process is to enjoy the present moment as much as possible. In fact, try to remove yourself from any worries or concerns about the past or future, and let yourself just enjoy right now.

Practice gratitude daily. Gratitude is a spiritual awakening technique that can be used in many different ways, but it can aid you to locate a sense of inner peace and happiness with life all on its own. Think about all the things in life that you truly appreciate and give thanks for those things every day. It's a great way to start your spiritual awakening process, and it's also a great way to make the process last longer.

Try to help others. You can also start your spiritual awakening by volunteering in ways that help others with their self-awareness and spiritual growth.

Balance Your Chakras. Having a balanced Chakra system in your body will allow you to accept the positive and pessimistic thoughts that go on in your mind, and at the same time, make you feel good inside. By balancing your Chakras, you can create a very peaceful and calm mind.

Spiritual awakening is your transition from being an ordinary person to a spiritually awakened individual. It is usually very different from what you might imagine. In your pursuit of spiritual awakening, you will come across many obstacles and challenges that will slow down or even stop you from achieving this goal. However, as long as you put in my mind the things that you have learned and you follow these steps, you'll find yourself on the path of true spiritual awakening.

Made in the USA
Monee, IL
05 August 2021